The Story of
Ron Rearick

ICEMAN

by Mari Hanes
and Ron Rearick

The Story of
Ron Rearick

Library of Congress Number 82-90708

ISBN 0-9609206-0-9

Editorial and Production: Falcon Press Publishing Co., Helena, Montana

Dedicated to
The Old Man

Contents

ICEMAN

1

The Million

Iceman sat motionless behind the wheel of his Camaro, scanning the horizon of the darkened Utah desert. He'd pulled off to the side of the two-lane highway a few miles south of Salt Lake City and headed the car up a slight incline until it was well hidden behind a ridge of boulders. From this vantage point, he watched for a car to cross the small bridge over the dry gully which was marked "Jordan River."

He was motionless, but not totally silent. His breath was coming hard and fast, almost in wheezes. "This ain't like me," he muttered aloud. "They don't call me Iceman for nothin'. It's all gone so smooth—just like I planned."

But he'd never pulled a job worth a million dollars either. And that's what he was waiting for that warm night in 1972—a million bucks.

Ron Rearick was 33 years old, of medium height and solid as a tank, with arms so muscular he looked like a professional wrestler. Keen blue eyes were habitually narrowed, glaring above a nose that had obviously been broken several times, yet somehow had healed without marring his rugged good looks. His square jaw was marked with a mouth set in a straight hard line, and every crease in his well-tanned face reinforced that hardness.

With the white light of the desert moon pouring over the coldness of his features, Ron appeared more than ever to be a man carved out of ice.

"Keep cool, Ron, keep cool," he muttered. "This gig is going like clockwork." To calm himself while he waited for the delivery of the million, he began to recall all of the planning, all of the details that had led to the climax of this brilliant scheme.

He remembered exactly when the idea had first hit him.

He had been sitting alone in the posh bar of the Stardust Hotel in Las Vegas, nursing a whiskey and brooding over the drug delivery he'd made that morning.

The pusher who had showed up to claim Ron's package of dope had been just a kid, probably working one of the high schools close to the Vegas Strip. The boy hadn't come with the amount of money that was expected, so Ron started to rough him up a little just to let him know that Rearick was no one to mess with. The punk had to learn that he was dealing with a Pro this time.

Then the guy had pulled a .22. Ron hadn't expected that kind of a weapon on such a young kid. Rearick moved like a cat to grab the pistol with a well-trained hand, then used to butt of the gun to beat a lesson into the boy. Next time—when he finally got healed up—that kid would show a lot more respect.

But the fight had unnerved Ron. He had made that delivery just for a little pocket money while he was in Vegas. He was used to this sort of action, but he was getting tired. Bone tired.

He was sick of all the hustle. Sick of always being on guard—always looking over his shoulder. Sick of the tremendous amount of mental energy it took for him to keep one step ahead of the cops and the competition. Sick of the physical effort it took just to stay alive.

"Oh, sure," he thought. "I've made lots of money. Thousands. Maybe hundreds of thousands in the last few years." But it had all slipped through his hands, and he was always having to hustle for more. After all, it took big bucks to maintain Ron's style of partying, his class of women, and his quality of dope!

Rearick had traveled to Nevada for time to think of a plan that would change his life. Sitting there in the Stardust bar, it came to him that he had just never gotten a large enough chunk of money at one time. If he had a big enough stash, he could buy into things higher up and live off the dividends. Maybe he would buy into condominiums. It was high time he left the risks to the beginners.

And Ron had an answer, a supply source for the huge amount he needed in one lump sum. It HAD to be the airlines. They were more loaded than any bank he could rob.

Several hijackings had been in the news in the first months of '72. Overseas, terrorist groups were using airline kidnappings for political causes. But in the U.S., hijack attempts had been made in Buffalo, in Sacramento, and in Oakland for a simpler cause: Money.

The attempts had failed. Those guys had been amateurs.

Ron knew that he had the connections to really score. He had contacts to help in the actual job, knowledge of explosives and the weapons it might take to deal with the Feds, and the connections to change the money and totally disappear when it was over.

Iceman left Vegas that very night, driving home to Salt Lake City to begin his preparation, his "research." Ron loved the research that it took to pull off one of his big jobs.

Then, when Stubs Riley had showed up in Salt Lake after a stint in Soledad Prison, Ron had decided it was fate. Now there was a guy with nerve. Ron and Stubs went way back. They'd met in the army, and together they'd pulled some pretty slick robberies and thrown some great parties.

Ole Stubs was the personification of his nickname. Squat, with stubs for arms, stubs for legs, and a stub for a torso. Even his hair was stubby. He'd kept it short ever since the army days, and it stuck up on top of his head in a bush GI.

"Come on, Man," Ron had told him a dozen times, "grow some hair. You're behind the times. No chicks want to date a scrub brush."

But Stubs was a crook cut from the red-neck mold. "I got my pride, Iceman. I ain't gonna look like no damned hippy!"

Ron trusted Stubs . . . well, trusted him as much as he trusted anyone. And as soon as he shared his plan, Stubs was ready to get in on the action.

Since Ron had most of the connections, he made it clear to Stubs that he would get the largest share of the money. After the usual foul-mouthed bargaining, they made their deal.

It had taken them four months to get ready.

Ron thought that the mistake the other hijackers had made was to try to take a plane while it was in the air. He figured it would be a lot easier to threaten to blow up a big one while it was in the terminal, just loaded for take-off and still attached to the building. Of course, he knew better than to risk getting the explosives on with a passenger. He arranged to have a bomb loaded with the luggage. And it just so happened that one of the loaders for United Airlines owed Ron a favor . . . a big one.

So the explosives were readied. The lay-out of the airport was studied and re-studied. The country roads around Salt Lake were scrutinized for the perfect drop-off point. Then Stubs made the trip back East to pick up their "fire power."

You see, it was evident to both of them that they would be dealing, not just with local cops, but with the Feds. No matter how quickly they could move the action, they'd be running into Feds. So they devised a plan to run the airlines delivery man from one phone booth to another while they observed to find out just how many FBI men were trailing the money. Then they planned to simply lie in wait in the desert and blow the Feds off the road.

It would take a "B.A.R."—a Browning Automatic Rifle. Stubs brought back a beauty from his trip East. Loaded on a heavy-duty tripod, it could pump rounds of ammo so rapidly that when they took it to the badlands to practice, it cut their large wooden targets in half. And for the day of the hijacking, they had purchased armor-piercing bullets.

Then Ron had a stroke of absolute genius that gave their plan a real touch of class.

In his research, Ron had run across a magazine article of United's executive offices in Salt Lake City. One picture showed a conference table, smiling white-shirted jerks all around it. Another photo showed the head of the Salt Lake City branch seated at his desk in a massive blue leather chair. Ron knew their phone calls for money would be more effective if they could describe those offices perfectly.

Both Stubs and Iceman were adept at breaking and entering, so access to the executive suite was not a great obstacle. They invaded the offices late on Friday night, and even enjoyed a picnic with the gourmet food they discovered in the executive refrigerator. They left the conference room in an absolute mess.

Then, just in the last two weeks, events in the nation had caused a change in their plans. There had been a rash of hijacking attempts; by the end of the year there would be 31 in the U.S. alone. Ron was furious. Some of those men were stealing his plans to operate from the ground!

But a smart man stays flexible, so Ron did some rethinking and told Stubs, "Hey, buddy, we've got it made!"

"The airlines are set up for us! Those dudes are running scared as rabbits from all the recent hijackings. We won't even have to risk getting caught while we load the bomb. We'll just tell them on the phone that we're sorry about the mess we left when we visited their offices. We'll drop hints that maybe we planted a bomb right on their doorstep.

They'll believe us! And we won't give them enough time to check."

So it was settled. Ron never even had to lean on his contacts within the airlines.

Stubs had made the phone calls. He had a great low voice for it. The first time, he had said only a few sentences . . .

"Mr. Jones, we've placed a remote controlled bomb on the #606 which has just loaded at Gate 11. Call them and tell them to freeze. No one gets off that plane, and no one else gets on. Just keep cool, and sit there in your big blue chair until you hear from me again. Oh, by the way, I'm sorry about the little mess we made when we visited your conference room." He hung up the receiver.

Stubs called Mr. Jones again from a different phone. Shaken by the understanding that the phone call had come from a man who had actually broken into the inner offices, Jones was ready to do business. The Airline had instructed him that if this situation ever arose, he was to take no chances on the lives of passengers. And he could see that these guys meant business.

"We want one million dollars, in hundred dollar bills, in exactly one hour. We won't negotiate, and this is the only time we'll ask. You are the delivery boy, Jones, don't send anyone else. Get the million in a flight bag and go to the phone booth at 21st and Temple. Don't you dare let them trail you."

Of course, Iceman and Stubs knew that he would be trailed. But they were ready.

Ron was parked in a supermarket lot adjacent to that phone booth. Exactly one hour later, Mr. Jones showed up . . . and he was carrying a white and blue flight bag.

The phone rang, and Stubs instructed Jones to leave his own car and get into the green Chevy parked at the corner with the keys in the ignition. Stubs told Jones to drive to the phone booth at Redwood Road and 13th Street South.

The schemers knew that at least two Feds were likely to be hiding on the floor of Jones' car. At least this way they had cut out some of the opponents.

Ron waited a few moments, memorizing the cars that followed within eyeshot of the green Chevy.

Jones showed up at the second booth; the phone rang and Stubs headed him to a third booth. When Jones pulled up to the third booth, Ron was already close by, waiting. Ron spotted the same brown sedan he had seen at the first booth checkpoint. Yep. There was only one car trailing Jones. In it sat three men, but probably three more were hidden.

Ron had then headed for his outpost above Highway 123, calling Stubs on the CB. "Hey, good buddy. I'm back from my hunting trip. But I only saw one muledeer."

Stubs had directed Jones toward the Jordan River overpass and told him to fling the airline bag over the right side of the bridge without even stopping his car. Stubs had made that last call from a gas station only two miles from the uninhabited area around the Jordan River gulch, so there had been plenty of time for him to get to where the B.A.R. had been set up in the cover of sagebrush a quarter mile before the drop-off point. Ron would grab the money and race to the nearby plateau where their twin engine Cessna was waiting. Ron would get the engine going while he waited for Stubs, the pilot.

After re-thinking the entire plan, Ron once again spoke to himself aloud. "Keep cool, man. It's goin' perfect!"

Just at that moment, car lights came into view on the horizon. Ron jumped and his heart stood still. He watched until he was certain that it was the green Chevy. Then, even from this distance up the hill, he clearly saw the large bag that was hurled over the edge of the bridge. The green car sped away. For a moment, the night was awesomely quiet.

Ron started his car and drove down the incline and back onto the road. He knew he had to move like lightning. The FBI trailing Jones would certainly be communicating their location to the cops continually right up to the place where Stubs lay in wait.

Ron jumped from his car and slid down the sandy creek bed with a loud Indian whoop. There it was! His Million! He felt the rare thrill, like he hadn't felt for ages. At last! His Million!

There had been no double-cross. In starchy hundred bills, luminous in the moonlight, lay one million dollars.

That moment to Ron, staring down at the million, seemed timeless. For in one split second, as soon as he actually saw his treasure, the wonderful thrill was gone.

"Oh, God!" he cursed. "It's not enough! It's not gonna be enough!

Iceman zipped up the bag and climbed back up the bank to his car, sputtering and swearing profusely. He threw the bag on the front seat by his .38 revolver, then turned the car toward the plateau and the small plane.

But anger was surging in Ron. Anger hot as molten lava. In a split second his dream had disintigrated right before his eyes, and he was bitterly disappointed. All the planning, all the chances they were taking for that money didn't even count. As soon as he saw it, he knew that even a million dollars wasn't going to satisfy him.

He felt his neck and face flush red with the force of his fury. In that moment of frustrated anger and hatred for the world and for all of life, Ron did a really stupid thing.

He slowed down. In fact, he stopped his car. He rolled down his window and sat there waiting. Listening.

He was waiting and listening to hear the explosion of gunfire that meant that Stubs and the Browning Automatic Rifle were blowing the Feds away.

Possessed by such anger and hatred, Iceman was aching to hear the sound of the FBI men being massacred. To his twisted, illogical rationale, it seemed like it would make up for some of his let-down. His million wasn't enough—and somebody had to pay.

He waited several long minutes. It was insane, but he waited. "Come on Stubs," he yelled into the heedless night, "let 'em have it!"

But no gunfire was heard.

"Now, Stubs, NOW!"

Still, not a sound.

"Damn it, Stubs!" he screamed, "I'm not leaving until I hear you blow them away!"

How had Ron Rearick become so hardened, so totally heartless? How can any man get to the place where he expects a measure of satisfaction from the bloody death of total strangers?

It had been a long road to that event in the Utah desert. It had taken years of violence and crime, of learning how to hate. It takes a lot to turn a man of flesh into a man of ice . . .

ICEMAN

2

The Chill Factor

A small boy's feet can move with pitiful slowness when he is headed in a direction he doesn't want to go. And nine-year-old Ron Rearick did not want to go to the new school.

As he shuffled down the main street of the little town of Rightwood, California, he thought how much alike the main streets of these mining towns were. In most, every other building was a tavern and the buildings between the taverns were establishments Pop called cat houses. There was always a dry goods store, filled with everything from Levi jeans to apples. And down at the end of main street, there was always an elementary school building with its dirt play-ground.

Still, within this pattern of sameness, Ron knew he had to face new teachers, new classes, and a new peer group made up of total strangers.

His family moved at least once a year; Pop often quit his job at one mine and headed off to a new mine, hoping for more money or a better position. The operation Pop joined in Rightwood was a lime mine, but there had been copper mines, silver mines—and once even a small gold claim that had stirred the man's ambitions.

Ron thought of his sister Violet, five years his senior, and wondered how she managed these transitions from one town to another. Even little Sue, five years younger, seemed to handle the moves better than Ron did. Well, maybe his sisters did mind the moves . . . but girls can cover their fears with a mask of feminine quietness.

"I wish Donnie had lived," Ron mumbled to himself. "We'd have been only two years apart in school, and we could've walked in together."

Ron still had a vivid memory of the trauma to his four-year-old heart when baby brother Donnie died of pneumonia one cold California winter.

Nearing the school yard, Ron wondered if even having a brother like Donnie would really help him. Momma still cried whenever they spoke of the child who had died, and whispered, "He was such an angel. And such a smart little boy!"

Ron didn't realize that mother had felt that about all of her babies. At age nine, all Ron knew was that he did not feel like a good boy. Or a smart boy.

Maybe it was because of Pop, bone-tired each night and usually drunk, was always pushing him away. Maybe it was because Ron was a part of the post-war baby boom, and started to school in classrooms so crowded that teachers had no time to spot a boy that was struggling and falling behind. From those first school days on, Ron thought of himself as dumb. Now, having been "passed" automatically at the end of each term, even though Ron was in grade four, he could barely read at all. The paragraphs in his text books looked like lines of mumbo-jumbo.

"Nope," Ron stated, "I ain't smart." And because of his ignorance, the boy couldn't be "good" either, for he had chosen to hide his ignorance with an outer shell of toughness.

Wrapping his covering of cool toughness around him, young Ron quickened his pace and strode into the front doors of the Adams Elementary School.

For three days, things went smoothly. Then came the first time Teacher called on Ron to answer a question in geography.

He didn't know the answer. His mouth went dry and his tongue felt thick, the way it did when it caused him to stutter and stammer. He wasn't about to offer an answer that might be wrong. He couldn't bear the smirks or the giggles classmates would aim at the new "dummy." So Ron immediately shifted everyone's attention from the arena of knowledge to the area in which he felt more comfortable—the arena of confrontation.

Ron glared at the teacher and spat out a string of cuss words.

Mrs. Conby's eyebrows shot up, her face reddened, and her finger pointed angrily to the door.

"Ron Rearick," she screamed, "get your body down to the Principal's Office this instant!"

Little did the instructor know that this was Ron's planned escape route. He would unflinchingly face swats with a ruler any day, rather than face the laughter or teasing of his peers.

His bold treatment of a teacher brought the new boy a measure of respect at Adams school. The children there were the usual mining town gang—most were rough products of rough home lives. But this new guy seemed to have more courage than they did. And the following week, Ron sealed his reputation as "a kid you don't mess with!"

During several recess periods, Ron had watched two brothers, Sam and Frank, as they picked on a smaller boy on the playground. It was obvious they had chosen a younger target because they were cowards and bullies who would only pick on the defenseless. One noon hour, Sam and Frank tripped the smaller boy, and then pushed his tearful face into a murky mud puddle.

Ron exploded. He felt powerful empathy for the weaker boy, as he always did when the "losers" of this world are put down by the "winners." He bolted onto Frank's back, knocked him to the ground, and kicked the wind out of the bully. Then Ron turned on Sam, banging his fist into Sam's surprised face, bloodying his nose and then blackening his eyes.

Suddenly a teacher loomed between Ron and his adversaries. All three boys were expelled, and told to return to school only if they brought their parents.

The harshest reprimands for that incident fell on Ron. Sam and Frank's dad owned the town's grocery store, and his influence swung the principal in his favor. Still, it was agreed that Ron could come back to school. And Ron's reputation at Adams was established. He was a darn good fighter! He had beaten two disliked bullies, both older and many pounds heavier than he was!

Boys in his class began to sit by Ron at lunch time, and he was now included in baseball and "Red Rover" at recess.

Ron's conscious and sub-conscious view of life began to crystallize during that year of his life. "Fear brings a measure of respect. It is better to be feared than to be laughed at."

In spite of these occasional eruptions and the constant seething dislike of his homeroom teacher, Ron would remember those days in Rightwood as the most carefree time in his life. For one thing, he was able to live there for one whole school year. He got to walk around town with buddies he'd known for a whole year!

Rightwood was pretty neat as mining towns go. There were lots of evergreen trees to adorn the streets, and just a few miles away a white mountain glistened and boasted a ski resort.

Some Friday afternoons the fourth, fifth and sixth graders were bused up the slopes for skiing lessons. Now those were great times! Struggling against the slippery snow was a great release for a young boy's pent up energy and anxiety.

There were a few incidents on the slopes, nothing major. Once Ron and his buddy Todd decided to "try out" some expensive racing skis that were leaning against the outside wall of the snack shop. Not realizing how noticable it would be, they tied those racers on over their street shoes and headed down the mountain towards home. When the snow grew scarce, they chucked the skis into some bushes and hitch-hiked on in.

Of course they had been seen. That night the Sheriff arrived at the Rearick cabin and demanded to know the whereabouts of those skis. When the Sheriff left, Ron received a hearty beating from his dad for "embarrassing the family." As Ron eased his bruised body into bed that night, he decided that the next time he "borrowed" something, he'd do a slicker job of it.

Opal and Oral Rearick

That year of 1949 Ron grew more husky with every pass-
ing month. By the time he turned ten years old, he was taller
than his mom. But as small and petite as Opal Rearick was,
Ron never thought of coming against her. Spry and quick-
moving, with flashing blue eyes and Irish temper, Opal was
battle-strengthened from years of withstanding the temperament of Ron's dad. Opal was affectionate to her children,
but it seemed as if the short woman was supported by an inner skeleton of iron. Ron knew that if he was within arms'
reach of her stinging slaps, he was in a position of real
danger!

And no one in the whole town dared to stand up to Pop.
Bearded, barrel-chested Oral Rearick was nicknamed Smiley
by the miners. "Smiley" was a title given sarcastically . . .
Mr. Rearick never smiled.

Ron was controlled when he was at home, in the shadow of
Opal and Oral. But that May he made a startling discovery
about the rest of the adult world.

Ron had kept his head down for months whenever Mrs.
Conby asked questions in the classroom. One Monday morning the inevitable happened. The teacher singled Ron out,
asking, "Ron, what is 5 x 5?"

Five times five. He thought he knew—25. But he needed
time to be more sure of his answer. Stalling, he bent down to
untie his tennis shoe and remove a rock that had slipped inside during morning recess. But as he stalled, Mrs. Conby
screamed at him . . .

"Ron! Don't take your shoe off in this classroom!"

"I got a rock in there, Teacher. I can't think while it's hurt-
ing," he replied.

"Listen, young man. If you take that shoe off in class, you
might as well get up and head out the door, and use those
shoes to keep right on walking."

Teacher was making an issue out of that shoe. Out of the
corner of his eye, to his great horror, Ron saw that two girls
sitting beside him were on the verge of laughter. Teacher
was undoing the respect it had taken months to acquire!

Barely knowing what he was doing, Ron picked up his
heavy math book and threw it straight at Mrs. Conby. The
stout woman was standing in front of her desk, hands on her
hips like a military sergeant. Thrown from such close range,
that big textbook slammed into her stomach like a cannon-
ball. Mrs. Conby grabbed her stomach and doubled over,
sinking to her knees.

As the class began chattering in amazement, Ron knew he
had to make a quick escape. He walked to the front of his

row in an embarrassed fury. He passed Mrs. Conby, still struggling to breathe and on her knees, and shoved her shoulders roughly. She fell forward in a heap.

Ron was out the door and headed down the hall before Mrs. Conby could draw in enough air to speak. But her husky voice echoed through the corridor after him.

"You will never get back in this school, Ron Rearick. Do you hear me? Never! Never!"

Ron was numb, barely able to put one foot in front of the other as he headed home. He had walked painfully slow the first time he headed toward Adams School. Now he walked even more slowly as he left for the last time.

As he plodded homeward, an awesome thought was sifting through the fog of his feelings. He had made a discovery. He was big enough now to hold his own, even against an adult.

"Nobody had better try to put me down, or embarrass me ever again." Ron was shivering so much that he barely got the words out. A north wind had swept down the valley, cutting through his worn-out coat and chilling him to the bone before he reached the cabin. "If they do, they'll be sorry."

ICEMAN

3

The Con Man

In 1953, Colton, California was the most troubled of the suburbs surrounding Los Angeles. It was here that Ron entered junior high school. (Pop had decided to try his hand at welding.) Colton was a different world from the small mining communities. Ron quickly absorbed the "in" styles of the city boy of L.A.: "pegged" pants, white T-shirts and black leather jackets. He combed his hair in a duck, called the girls "tweeks" and sauntered like James Dean, his movie idol.

The schools in Colton were subdivided into street gangs. There were constant gang clashes, or "rumbles." Whites against blacks. Blacks against Chicanos. Chicanos against Orientals.

Ron was involved in his usual private rumbles. The second day at the junior high, Ron got confused and ended up in the wrong homeroom. When his name was called during roll, the boy across from him made a smart aleck remark. With a quick right swing, Ron knocked him clear out of his seat. And was promptly expelled for three days.

He found his first girlfriend that month. Dimpled, blonde Marilyn was a real catch. He captured her heart as she was putting her coat into her locker. A tall ninth grader walked by and slapped her on the bottom. She turned around, face flushed with anger and embarrassment, just in time to see

Ron deck the offender. "Ronnie" immediately became her knight in shining armor.

The ninth grader turned out to be the leader of one of the school's gangs. That night after school he challenged Ron to a one-on-one fight, threatening to kill Ron as his gang looked on. It was a big mistake. Ron beat the boy bloody.

As the word of Ron's fighting ability spread, he was courted by several of the gangs. "I'll think on it. Don't rush me," he always said. But in his heart, Ron knew he'd never join any of them. He didn't think it took much courage to fight or run in a pack. He'd rather make it on his own . . . not bossed by them, not dependent on them.

He carried that attitude with him to manhood. Years later, even pressure from the world-famous Hell's Angels could not persuade him to join them; but they would respect him and allow him to operate in their turf as a lone wolf.

In the seventh grade, Ron still held to a boyish inner code of what he though was right and what he thought was wrong.

In Ron's code of ethics, it was all right to fight if someone laughed at him.

It was all right to fight if someone strong picked on someone weaker, such as the boy on the Rightwood playground or a girl like Marilyn.

It was all right to fight when you were openly challenged by someone in power, such as a gang leader . . . or an adult.

But it was wrong to take advantage of anyone, to act like a bully, or to pick a fight just for the sake of fighting.

Ron still had a heart of flesh, a heart able to feel the pain of others and to empathize with that pain.

The most violent event of his early teens happened because of that empathy.

Jerry was a friendly kid in several of Ron's classes. He was a real egghead, overweight and hidden behind thick black-rimmed glasses. "Kind of a dip, but a good Joe," Ron thought. Every day, Jerry happily loaned Ron notebook paper, pencils, and other supplies (Ron never had any of his own).

One night after school, two upper class gang members caught Jerry alone in the locker room. For no reason other than meanness, they attacked the "egghead," beating him unmercifully and giving Jerry a concussion.

The next morning in class, Ron discovered that Jerry was in the hospital in a coma. His right side would often twitch with spasms, and if Jerry came out of the coma, the doctors feared paralysis.

Ron was sick all over. He went to the restroom and vomited until he could hardly stand, and his skin felt clammy and cold. Why did it have to be Jerry who was hurt so badly, a boy who never made fun of anyone or put anyone down? And what two guys were such cowards that they would gang up on such a pitiful target?

Ron determined to find out and do something about it.

Those in authority in a school system may never know the source of problems, but it doesn't take long for the students to find out. Ron simply kept his ears open and before the week was over had learned which two ninth graders were bragging that they had "nearly killed someone with their bare hands."

Ron knew which of the lavatories those boys used each morning for a smoke break. Friday morning Ron didn't go to class—he went to the gymnasium and stole a baseball bat. Then he went to the lavatory, hid in one of the stalls, and he simply waited.

In a matter of minutes, the two offenders sauntered into the bathroom. Only four feet away from Ron's hiding place, they actually were joking about how tough they had been on Jerry! Their callousness was too much for Ron; he burst out of the stall and attacked them like an angel of judgment.

Ron smashed the bat into the back of one of the boys before the kid could turn around. His first blow cracked two ribs, and his next downward swing broke the boy's jaw.

The other boy screamed and threw his arms across his face to protect himself. The bat of fury dislocated his shoulder, and as his arm dangled helplessly, smashed into his face and shattered his nose.

Ron ran out of the bathroom, tossed the bloody bat into a garbage can, and calmly walked to class. Meekly, he asked the teacher to excuse him for being late.

That afternoon Ron was called to the principal's office, where a policeman was waiting. Calmed by feeling like an avenger, Ron told the officer that these were the two boys who had put his friend, Jerry, in the hospital. Ron implied that the two had been waiting in the bathroom with a stolen bat to threaten him and scare him into not "squealing," but that he had been able to grab the bat and defend himself.

The officer believed Ron. After all, what seventh grader would be fool enough to go against two ninth graders? And besides that, Jerry had miraculously come out of the coma that same day, and identified his two assailants. The incident was closed, and Ron felt extremely proud of himself.

In the eighth grade, Ron opened his first business.

The guys at school were always involved in small thefts. Ron would see them rip off candy bars from the snack counter, or pop from the corner store. But Ron's ideas for getting things that he wanted or needed didn't run in the ordinary pattern. Maybe it was because Ron was so well-acquainted with his mom's brother, Uncle Mick. Uncle Mick was a con man, a REAL con man.

Uncle Mick viewed life as one long poker game filled with bluffing and trickery. Mick had gotten money out of "unsuspecting suckers" in more ways than can be recounted. Ron thought of Mick like Pop did. Mick was a genius!

In eighth grade, bored with text books that he could not read anyhow, Ron began to spend hours in the classroom daydreaming about ways to make money. Lots of money. Enough to go to the show every weekend if he wanted, even enough to take Marilyn and buy her whatever she desired.

With a friend called Doby, he went into the newspaper business.

Ron and Doby would buy one new Sunday paper, and separate it into individual sheets. They then would wrap the new sheets around old newpapers that they had collected from garbage cans. Peddled door to door, the old newspapers netted a quarter apiece.

Often Ron and Doby sold the papers at the train station to commuters who leaned out through the windows. The adults would often pay for the paper with a dollar bill or a five, and since the trains stopped only for a minute, Ron and Doby could hang onto the bills and wave good bye with grins as trains pulled away and angry men yelled for their change.

One day at work, Smiley Rearick encountered a sarcastic foreman.

"I'm surprised to see you still working here, Rearick," the foreman said.

"What do you mean?" Smiley asked.

"Well, with all the money your boy's made selling our neighborhood used newspapers, I thought you could retire by now!" came the icy reply. "You must be a wealthy man with a con man like Ron for a son!"

Smiley had been disgraced in front of his fellow workers.

The welts he laid on Ron that night lasted for days. It was the end of a brilliant newspaper career.

One Saturday night Doby and Ron were out after curfew, just "hanging out" in the city and looking for something to do. As they passed a darkened alley, they jumped at the sight of a uniformed policeman, and hid themselves before they were hauled home. They watched the cop in amazement. He was bent over a drunk who had passed out in the alley; he searched the drunk and stuffed all of the man's money and valuables into his own pockets!

Ron's eyes widened at this instantaneous revelation. So even some cops are lawbreakers, he thought. Con men.

As the policeman stood up, he saw the two boys. Ron and Doby started to flee, but Ron changed his mind and stood his ground.

"We know what you've been up to, Man," Ron was glaring at the officer. "We want in on the action."

So in they were. Within a few nights, Officer Cooper knew he had formed a good partnership. With Ron and Doby standing guard on the streets, he was able to move much more quickly in his business in the alleys. He kept most of the big bills, but the kids turned a good profit, too. For an entire summer, 13-year-old Ron Rearick was in the business of "rolling" drunks.

Then one night, one of the drunks turned out to be another policeman in disguise. He surprised the crooked cop and quickly overpowered him. At the same time, Ron and Doby were nailed in the street by another plainclothesman. The three were immediately booked into the Los Angeles County Jail.

Officer Cooper was tried swiftly and sentenced harshly. He had not only committed felonies, he was an officer of the law who had involved minors in those felonies. He was given 55 years in the State Pen.

Ron and Doby waited for their hearings in the cells of the juvenile detention center. A jail in itself, the center held young men charged with everything from car theft to murder. In self-defense, Ron acquired even more hard meanness, and more tricks for "dirty fighting."

Ron Rearick's inner and outer selves at that time were a confused jumble of meanness and pity, of what seemed right and what seemed wrong. It had seemed wrong for other boys to pick on Jerry the egghead. But it seemed all right to steal from the drunks. After all, they were adults who should have known better than to pass out in an alley with money in their pockets.

Ron desperately wanted some love, some feelings left in his life . . . but it seemed hard to combine that with the toughness he was going to need to "get by" in the jungle called life. At no time was his dilemma more graphic than the day Mom Opal came to visit him in Juvenile Hall.

After only 48 hours, Ron had established himself as a tough dude that nobody planned to mess with. Then in marched Opal. In her hands she carried a giant five-layered german chocolate cake.

How she had talked the guard into letting her enter the cell block with that cake he couldn't imagine. And her Irish temperament had even pushed him into letting her enter with a long butcher knife with which to cut the cake!

"Hello, Son," she said simply. With no mention of Ron's trouble, she proceeded to cut huge slices of that cake and distribute them to the six boys in the cell. Six mouths hung open in amazement, then grinned in gratitude. Her task completed, Opal caught Ron in a strong bear hug, took up her empty plate and butcher knife, and left without another word.

Ron grimaced. Now how can a guy maintain his image with a mom who pulls a stunt like that?

But the cake lay in his stomach, filling . . . and comforting.

4

The Dealer

Cooper had received 55 years in prison. Ron figured that he and Doby would spend the rest of their teen years at the state reformatory. But when their sentence came, it was surprisingly light. The boys were so young that the judge felt certain they were coerced into crime by the crooked policeman. By summer, Ron was back on the streets.

The Rearick clan was on the road once more. This time they landed in Farmington, New Mexico, so Pop could be near the oil and uranium mines.

After the trouble in Colton, Ron was glad to be in a smaller town once again. He knew what to expect from other "miner's brats" and made friends quickly. With several older guys he met on the streets, Ron signed up for a two-week-long National Guard Training Camp. Of course he was only 14, but so muscular and tough that he easily passed for 16.

The Guard camp was located in El Paso, Texas, just minutes from the Mexican border. It was this fact that prompted Ron and his buddies to join. They had heard of the high times that could be had in Juarez for just a few bucks—the cheap booze and the ample supply of street girls. The reports were all true.

Every night, Ron slipped from his tent, walked across the border, and made the rounds of the Mexican bars. Then, just before dawn, he and the gang crept back into their pup tents for an hour or two of shut-eye before reveille sounded.

There were days when they were deathly ill from the strong varieties of Mexican brew. And there was one night when Ron almost got himself stabbed. He put his arm around the wrong prostitute. Her Spanish lover was close by and pulled out a switchblade. Luckily, he was drunker than Ron, and was easily knocked out. But all in all, the boys thought they were really living.

When Ron returned from camp and moved with his parents to Moab, Utah, he no longer felt like a kid. At 14, he thought of himself as a man.

Moab was like a frontier town out of a television western. Wood-framed buildings rose out of a sandy prairie rolling with tumble weeds. The crews that worked the mine were the rowdiest Ron had ever seen. Fights broke out round the clock in the three saloons, and often there were stabbings and shoot-outs.

In 1955, Ron announced that he would go to school no longer. Opal protested, but gave in. She knew her son would only be in class for a few days, anyhow, before he would be expelled. Pop was drinking when Ron told them. He turned bloodshot eyes to Ron and gave a slurred command.

"Then from now on, you earn your own way. If you're gonna sleep under my roof you can come to work in the mines like the rest of us!"

"Fine," Ron growled in answer.

He went to work in the uranium mine, running a jackhammer. He worked fast and hard and held his own. "But I won't be in this sweat trap for long," he told himself. "Pop has worked like an animal all these years and it got him nowhere."

At night, he still had enough youthful, restless energy to head for a saloon to drink beer and play cards. He was never even asked to show I.D.

His favorite hangout was "The Bluebird" saloon because of the illegal poker games that went on in the back room. When the owner of the joint learned to trust Ron he was allowed to watch. But Ron didn't play—the stakes were way too high.

One night the dealer, a boy from Salt Lake City, was accused of cheating. A surly miner held a pistol to his head. The owner, Jake, cooly returned all the money taken in the last few hands and the game broke up for the night. But the dealer was unnerved. "That does it! I quit!" the young man spat out his decision as he walked out the door.

Ron seized the opportunity. "Can I try it, Jake?"

"Sure," came the answer. "I ain't got no one else. If you deal for me tomorrow night I'll pay the usual $75.

The next night, Ron began his career as a dealer. He was good, really good, and Jake was pleased. Pop labored all day in the mine for peanuts compared to this; by the time he turned 15, Ron's daily earnings were three times the amount earned by his dad.

Ron began to spend almost all of his time at the Bluebird, shooting pool, drinking, even fighting if the need arose. He had plenty of dough, so whenever he got hungry he simply walked across the street and ordered a big steak at the best cafe in town.

The diner was called "Rose's." But the waitress and cook was named Clarissa.

Clarissa was 21, half-Mexican, half-Indian, and totally beautiful. Clarissa knew how to tease, how to laugh, and how to listen. For the first time in his life, Ron talked with someone for hours.

Clarissa was married. Her husband worked the night shift at the mine seven days a week, greedy for overtime pay. "Oh, Ron," she confided, "I am a very lonely woman."

Ron found he couldn't stay away from Rose's Cafe. He began to wonder how he could possibly ask a married woman out, and even if he asked her, where they could go. Late one Monday night no one showed up to play blackjack, so Ron eagerly went across the street to order a steak and be near Clarissa. He started to tell her how much he wanted to take her somewhere classy . . . but before he even finished his sentence, she asked him to come upstairs to her apartment.

Their relationship lasted for six months. He never mentioned his age, and he loved Clarissa with the intensity of a man twice his age. He constantly told her he loved her, believing that she loved him. He begged her to run away with him and become his wife.

Then one day Ron learned Clarissa had been badly beaten by her husband, Phil. Seething with anger, Ron sat at a bar wondering where he could get a gun to go kill the guy. Then Ron heard the rest of the story. Clarissa's husband had found a man's watch in the apartment, a watch belonging to Phil's boss. Clarissa haughtily told him that she had been entertaining many nighttime guests.

MANY. The word burned into Ron's heart as if he had been branded.

"Fool," he called himself. "Idiot." How could he have thought a woman could be trusted any more than the men he knew? Why had he believed her words of love?

With an act of his will, Ron turned his feelings of love into hatred. But the hurt of that first romance lasted for a long, long time.

ICEMAN

5

Knifed in the Heart

Clarissa left town. Ron continued his nightly job as the dealer at the Bluebird. He took some of the earnings home to Mom and Pop, but most of his money was eaten away by drinking and gambling. Already, Ron had become as much of an alcoholic as his father.

Besides his good pay from Jake, Ron picked up a little extra dough in another enterprise. Ron had put up the needed cash when a friend wanted to bring a couple of prostitutes to town, which made him part owner of the business. Ron also dipped his hand into Jake's till regularly. He figured Jake owed him; after all, Ron served as bouncer for the joint, too.

Ron was involved in violent fights more and more often. It was not unusual for a quarrel to break out over a game of pool or darts, and Ron would have to knock miners' heads together and send them on their way. Other fights began simply because of the reputation he had built for himself as a champion street fighter. Total strangers would enter the bar and curse Ron to arouse his anger and begin a brawl.

In those instances, Ron would become a crazy man, almost blind with uncontrollable hatred and anger. He had never been a "clean" fighter (why fight at all unless you planned to come out on top), but now he became ruthless. He would use a pool stick, a broken bottle, or whatever else was handy to deal with his opponent. More and more, a spirit of violence seemed to possess him. Once a brawl began, all reason left him and he wanted to destroy, to kill.

The empathy, "fighting for the underdog," which had once been a part of his personality, was now gone. Mercy cannot co-exist with seething hatred. The life Ron had lived in the past few years had acted as a knife in his heart, stabbing deep and draining away his supply of human emotion. Ron was in transition, changing from a man who was tough to a man who was truly dangerous.

Opal and Smiley Rearick were leaving Moab, moving to Salt Lake City. Ron decided that he needed a change, too. Dipping his hand into Jake's cash for a farewell bonus, he waved good-bye to the job as a dealer and headed south. Ron and two pals had decided to go on a cross-country tour.

"After all, there's a lot of places to see," Ron told himself, "and whatever we need, we can steal as we go."

What Ron, Lee Williams and Chad Barker called a cross-country tour became in reality a cross-country robbing spree. Through Utah and Nevada and Arizona, down to Texas and then up to Oklahoma, the three young men drank and brawled their way through dozens of towns. Their youth made them feel invincible, and they teased each other about becoming television stars on the popular series, "Route 66."

The "jobs" they pulled were usually small ones, and they managed to keep ahead of the law. Only once did the police throw them in the cooler, and then only for drunk driving. The three really were "sweating it" during that weekend in jail; beneath the back seat of their car was a treasure chest of loose change which Chad had "collected" from cigarette and pop machines. But the car was not searched—that Monday they were released.

Finally, they grew tired of the road and tired of one another. Ron located a cousin, Jack, and Jack invited Ron to share his apartment.

Jack worked for a company that ran oil rigs, and within a week Ron had found a job there, too. Ron liked those months of his life; the men on the oil rigs were tough and hard-working and he felt like one of them. Without realizing it, Ron began to feel NORMAL. He could turn on a great personality when he wanted to, and he became an extrovert in this place where no one knew that he could not read or write. The oil workers drank and gambled and cursed like he did, but they also had wives and families and were settled. Ron began to realize that he was on his own now; he could stay in one place and keep the same friends for the rest of his life, if he wanted.

And then Ron met Anna.

Tall and slender, Anna was a striking woman. Her Scandanavian heritage showed in her finely chisled features and blond hair. Ron first saw her across the dance floor at a company party. She had come in with another oil worker; she left with Ron.

Anna looked sophisticated, "cool," but she had a great sense of humor. She was a real party girl, although she never joined Ron in drunkenness. A great many of their dates included huge suppers she cooked for him.

Soon Ron could tell that Anna wanted to marry him. "Why not?" he thought. "I've already sown my share of wild oats." Though just 18, he felt much older. He was tired of picking up chicks at bars, tired of dates who didn't know his last name or a thing about him.

In March 1959 he and Anna eloped.

"Look at me!" he grinned inwardly in those first weeks of married life, "Ron Rearick is a normal guy!" He and Anna did their share of fighting, but they made up passionately. Within the year, baby Kathy was born.

Ron did fairly well at living the "normal" life until baby Kathy was about six months old. Of course, he had never stopped smoking and drinking. . .but he had certainly cut back. Gambling and hitting the bars was only for weekends in the first months of married life. Friday, Saturday and Sunday nights he partied, but Monday through Thursday nights he did his drinking at home.

In their second year of marriage, though, Ron found himself so restless when he was home that life with Anna became one long quarrel. He screamed at his wife and she screamed back. He often hit her. Little Kathy's constant crying set him on edge. Kathy was a pretty baby, but even his own daughter didn't fill Ron's heart with the love he had expected to feel.

Even his marriage would be better off, Ron decided, if he went back to "being himself." Being himself meant barhopping every night.

One Tuesday Ron drove to the neighboring town of Norman for a hot game of poker. Ron was good at cards, real good, but that night some "turkey" from Reno was picking up every hand. Ron had been paid that day—$70 for a week of working the rigs—and he lost it all. He knew Anna was counting on that money for groceries.

Driving home, drunk but coherent, Ron became increasingly angry. That Reno dude had taken his money from him! Well, Ron would not go home until he had gotten his paycheck back!

Ron had been carrying a gun in his car, hidden under his seat, ever since the cross-country spree. He reached for the revolver and there it was, loaded and ready. Anger instead of cunning directed his actions; he pulled in at the first market he came to on the country road that headed to Oklahoma City.

It was a small grocery business that included a late-night drug store. The owners, an elderly man and his wife, were just closing the cash register when Ron strode into the building. They looked up to greet him, and then froze in terror at the sight of the gun.

"Open that register and put all the money in a bag," Ron commanded.

"Yes, Sonny," the old man answered slowly. He opened the machine, and his frail wrinkled fingers scooped everything from its drawer.

Ron looked into the sack he was handed. At least two hundred, he thought. Then he had another idea. Stores this far from a bank usually had their own safe."

He held the revolver to the old man's head. "Now take me to your safe!"

"Tell him, Daddy, tell him where it is!" the little grandmother was pleading.

"It's over there." The man pointed the way. And as Ron held the gun high, the elderly woman pushed aside a large shelf of hairsprays and shampoos, and worked the safe's combination.

Ron saw clearly that what he had discovered was a vault housing many weeks of earnings. He began to drop piles of paper bills into a large grocery bag.

The old man and woman looked heartbroken, but calm. Ron was so angry that night that he would have harmed them. But as the elderly couple stood holding hands, his anger seemed to subside. They were very weak and vulnerable. "What am I doing picking on someone like them?" he thought.

Not knowing why he did it, Ron handed the man the bag and said, "Now. You count out $70. I need my grocery money."

The old man looked incredulous, but he obeyed. Ron stuffed the $70 in his pocket, then walked to the door of the store without reclaiming the bag. He looked at them one last time. "I'm not gonna tie ya or knock ya out," he spat. "But don't you dare call the cops, or I'll be back and find ya."

As he hurried from the store, he heard the old man say the

most ridiculous thing: "Praise the Lord, we're all right. Now, Momma, we had better pray for that poor boy . . ."

Ron put the stolen cash on the kitchen table, and slid into bed beside a sleeping Anna. He lay awake all night, totally sober and realizing what he was becoming. Once he had had some sort of a code of ethics; now he picked on anyone. He didn't even seem to feel much for his own wife and kid. And at 20, he was so achingly bored with living that he felt he was choking to death.

"What will help is a change of scenery!" thought Ron. "This bend-in-the-road called a town is driving me nuts. We need some city life. Some excitement."

That morning he commanded Anna to start packing. "We're moving to Oakland, California," he told her.

They left the next day.

ICEMAN

6

Hell's Angels

"You are not treating little Kathy like you should. I will not stand by and see my own grandbaby mistreated!" Anna's father, Thor Sorenson, was shaking his big fist in Ron's face. Grampa's words were thickened by his heavy Scandinavian accent. "And you are no good for my daughter, either."

"I have never hurt my kid!" Ron yelled. He slammed his hand against a table to keep from slamming it into his father-in-law's face.

"No, but you might. Any night in one of your drunken fits you could harm Kathy. She's such a frail little tyke."

"I suppose you think they'd be better off without me! Is that what you're saying, Thor?"

"Yes," the aging man nodded. "The way you are now, they'd be better off without you."

"All right." Ron lowered his voice. Instead of yelling, he spoke in tones cold and emotionless. "Then you take care of them from now on."

Ron turned his heel and walked out the front door of the Sorenson bungalow. The move to Oakland had been planned to bring back some joy to life and maybe help his marriage, but the move had also put them close to Anna's parents. Ron blamed their final break-up on "interference" by these in-laws. Yet as he walked away that spring morning, he didn't even feel sorry.

Living in Oakland, Ron came in touch with what he called "my kind of people." The guys and gals he got to know in an area of town around Seventh Avenue were bold and outspoken, ready for anything. Most of these new friends belonged to the infamous Hell's Angels.

Ron began working as the bouncer for the Top Hat nightclub. It was here that he met a new lady friend, a platinum blonde named Sandy. She was working in a topless joint when he first found her, but she let him know right away that that wasn't her best line of work. Sandy was a thief of extraordinary boldness.

Before long she and Ron were hitting jewelry stores up and down the California coast. They had a great operation; Ron and Sandy would pretend to be an engaged couple and ask to see a tray of diamonds. As they looked over the diamonds, two friends would begin a fist fight at the front of the store. When the employees rushed to settle the fight, Sandy and Ron quickly exchanged several of the rings on the tray with dimestore phonies Sandy carried in her purse. When the employees returned to serve them, they simply said they were going home to talk over a selection, and waltzed out with thousands of dollars of merchandise.

The greatness of the plan was that the thefts usually weren't noticed until other customers had looked over the trays. By that time, Ron had had the diamonds reset by his jewel connection.

After several months in Oakland, Ron had such an expensive drug habit that it took constant robberies to support his desire for high grade coke (cocaine) and pot (marijuana). Of course he had tried drugs before, marijuana in high school and acid (LSD) once or twice in the bars. But in the Bay Area, dope was so easily obtained that it became more important to Ron than booze.

He and Sandy did so much stealing that summer that Ron began to think of things he wanted as HIS even before they were in his possession. Once they stood beside an Oriental businessman at a store counter and saw him pull out a wallet that was literally stuffed with hundred dollar bills. Ron decided to follow him and "lift" that wallet.

As they tailed the man, he walked into a jewelry store, purchased an expensive watch, and paid for it in cash. "He's spending MY money!" Ron thought. Then the man left the watch to be engraved. "I won't even be able to lift the watch off that turkey now," Ron groaned. Then the stranger headed on down the boulevard.

As the man neared an alley, Ron closed in, pushed him into the side street and knocked him out cold before he uttered a sound. Sandy grabbed the wallet. There were still several hundred left, but not near as much as Ron had hoped for. Rearick gave the man an extra kick for spending his money.

This thought-pattern made sense in Ron's twisted lifestyle.

Frenchie Peterson, one of the pack of bikers named Hell's Angels, continually urged Ron to "join." But Ron was basically a loner. In reality, he didn't need a gang. Sometimes he felt he had the anger and brute force of an entire "gang" inside him. Once when he mentioned that to a bartender, the guy asked Ron if he had ever heard the story in the Bible of a man called Legion. Ron answered with a simple, truthful, "No."

Ron was glad for his contact with the Angels when it came time to party. There were lots of weekends when Ron knew he would go absolutely crazy if he had to be alone. The gang members were always planning one huge dope orgy after another.

One night in October of 1962, Ron learned that Sandy lived next door to a man who ordered pharmaceutical supplies for drugstores in the area. Sandy had watched Mr. Cole leave for work with display cases and trays filled with pills—-samples to be shown to druggists. Ron knew that if he stole this huge supply of samples, he would have enough "uppers" and "downers" to host a fantastic party!

The next morning when Cole got into his car, Ron was waiting for him on the floor of the back seat. When Ron shoved a sawed-off shotgun against the back of Cole's neck, the man began to shake and Ron knew intuitively he didn't even carry a gun to protect his valuable cargo. Rearick simply picked up the trays and left, telling the shaken salesman that he would blow his brains out if he turned around to get a description for the police.

Sandy got the telephone grapevine going, and Ron felt like the millionaire owner of a country estate as they gave invitations to a weekend at his place, "drink and dope on the house." It was this party, and not an actual theft or mugging, that gave Ron his first real criminal record and stint in prison.

Ron's rented house was the pad where two groups of bikers and assorted street people converged for a "grand bash." Rock music blared from open windows, huge choppers filled the lawn and overflowed onto the street, and shrieks and demonic laughter could be heard for blocks.

Ron had filled the refrigerator and a dozen ice chests with booze, and spread the trays of pills across the dining table.

"Serve yourselves, buffet style," he laughed and pointed to the drugs whenever a newcomer arrived. The guests could identify the pills they were popping by their shapes and sizes.

As the night went on, the party grew louder. It was inevitable that the police would be summoned.

What the patrolmen found was one of the largest drug parties ever reported. With several carloads of reinforcements, the officers entered Ron's home and found a massive stash of over-the-counter drugs. Chicks and some bikers split across the back lawn while others stayed to fight with chains and clubs.

Ron, Frenchie and several other Angels were hustled into a paddy wagon. Strong steel mesh separated them from the cops in the front seat. As Ron sat seething in the "jail car," he felt the violence, like a gang from within, bring him to the boiling point. Then, just outside the vehicle, he saw an officer smack a downed biker in the head with a billy club.

Ron leaned back in his seat, lifted his legs against the meshwork and with insane brute force kicked the restraining wall so that it popped out of the roof and crashed onto the heads of the policemen. The other men jumped forward into the seat and out of the paddy wagon, but Ron grabbed the neck of the driver, almost strangling him before help arrived.

Ron was charged with possession of narcotics. Yet it seemed to him that the real thorn in the flesh of the lawmen was that he had single-handedly messed up their paddy wagon. He was sentenced to time in the state pen in Tracy, California.

Tracy Prison is described as a "gladiator school." Ron was involved in so many fights in the yard that he was sure his sentence would be extended. He also lived with the constant danger that some of his past crimes would be traced.

He had been in jail often, but prison time was "another ballgame." Instinctively, Ron learned the ropes. He learned that you survive mentally in the pen by doing one day at a time, and by closing your mind to the outside world. He learned to read the character of the other inmates. He lived by the three cardinal rules for serving time; you hear nothing, you see nothing, you tell nothing.

The only thing about Tracy that really unnerved him was the racial clashes. He had never thought much of color differences, but in prison he HAD to. Ron knew he could defend himself one-on-one, but when large ethnic groups were clashing, every man in the joint was in danger.

After two and a half years, Ron was eligible for parole.

Soon he was home in Salt Lake City. He spent several weeks just lying beside the pool at the new apartment he rented. He could barely stay indoors for more than an hour; the sun and desert wind convinced him that he was a free man. There was no one to tell him where to go or what to do.

That wasn't true for long. Ron had just started to work for a freight company when he received his draft notice. His new warden was the United States Army.

ICEMAN

7

Failure to Adjust

Ron Rearick had never seen anything that affected him like the glistening blanket of winter that lay heavy on the evergreens of Northern Germany. He'd gone to boot camp at Ford Ord, then spent a few weeks at Fort Dix expecting to be sent to Korea. But orders had come through for Germany, and he had stepped off the air transport into a winter wonderland of European landscape that was awesome.

He remembered the good times he had had as a boy in Rightwood during the school's ski lessons. The snow there had been confined to a single mountain top. This snow extended from the mountains to the valleys to the plains. It softened the harsh angles of buildings and covered streets that might have looked ordinary or dingy without a clean, glistening garment. That blanket of snow filled his heart with a vague sense of yearning that he could not understand.

In April, the snow began to melt. The spring thaw turned the roadways into slippery mudways, and wherever patches of snow remained they were gray and ugly.

Ron sank into a sullen depression. The landscape reminded Ron of himself. He had once tried to cover his inner turmoil with a "normal" lifestyle, with a wife and a baby and an eight-to-five job that made him look different for a little while. But then that "normal" image had melted, and the ugly, real Ron Rearick had shown through. He hadn't been able to love his wife, or even his baby.

The routine of Army life didn't keep Ron busy enough to stop him from thinking, and real partying could only be done on leave. There was always "business" to be done, so Ron kept himself occupied with his usual lucrative business ventures.

His number one business was black-marketing. The American goods which were available on the base brought high prices in the German hamlets. Ron and other G.I.s could buy a carton of cigarettes in the PX for $1.50 and sell it for $5.00 in town. A bottle of whiskey from home cost $2.75 and could be sold for $35.00. Black marketers made huge profits on anything and everything, from warm winter clothing to gasoline.

Many base products were available only by using ration cards, but men who were really racketeers made use of many ration cards besides their own.

Ron got dozens of ration cards because of his second business. He cornered the market on loan sharking.

A loan shark provides money to guys who need it, short-term and high interest. A loan shark was already well-established when Ron arrived at Wieldflichen; he loaned $10 and required $20 in return, or loaned $20 and required $40 in return. Ron began his banking by loaning out $10s and only requiring $15 in return. It wasn't long before he stirred the anger of the competition.

"Look, buster, you ain't messing with some backwoods idiot. Did you think I'd let you come in and ruin my business? If you make even one more loan I'm gonna break your neck." The hulk of a Sergeant who cornered Ron in the chow line made his threat through clenched teeth.

"Do you understand?" he asked.

"Sure, man," Ron answered slowly, and stretched his lips into a phony smile. "I understand."

Rearick knew better than to lay into the man in the mess hall and end up with time in the brig. He'd choose his own time to deal with the jerk.

The time was that very night. Ron found Sergeant Rayburn sitting in a bar in town. Rearick unleashed his violent temper before Rayburn even knew he was there. The man was far heavier than Ron, but he did not have Ron's background in dirty brawling. In minutes, Ron finished him off, picked him up by the lapels and threw him out of the bar's plate glass window.

Another rough G.I. stood outside of that window, watching the fight and grinning with excitement. When Sergeant

Rayburn broke through the glass and lay in a bloody heap on the street, this soldier picked the man up and shoved him back in through the window.

"Hey, Mister, did you drop something?" the G.I. asked Ron with a smirk.

"Guess I did," Ron laughed. This stranger obviously appreciated a good brawl. Ron picked Rayburn up and, once again, threw him through the window into the street. "Oops!" he kidded, "dropped him again."

The soldier tossed Rayburn back inside, and Ron and he continued this private joke by exchanging the limp body several times. It seemed like a game of ping pong, or tennis. Then Ron broke out laughing, and invited the stranger in for a drink.

This was how Ron cornered the loan shark business. This was also how he met his army buddy, the soldier nicknamed Stubs.

With a soul mate like Stubs, a guy who wasn't afraid to back up threats for late payment with angry muscle, Ron became the loan shark for the entire base. Of course, he immediately raised his interest rate to 100%. If G.I.s couldn't come up with the cash, they would fork over their ration cards. Then Ron and Stubs moved into bigger and better business—drug running.

Hashish, or "hash," was plentiful in Germany, being brought in through Holland. High grade dope from Amsterdam could be obtained by trading whiskey from the base. Soon, however, Ron and Stubs had enough capital to deal only in cash and were able to supply the soldiers with heroin.

Ron's dealings in dope were so ruthless, so cold and calculated, that he earned his own nickname. The Iceman. It described him perfectly, so perfectly in fact that it was used more than his own name for the next 10 years.

In October, Ron's battalion was ordered to the field on manuevers. With thousands of other soldiers, Ron spent six weeks creeping across Germany on his hands and knees, through mud, briars and gunfire, in what the military honorably calls "war games."

The only food to be had was C rations which were delivered in "personnel carriers," transport vehicles on racks which resembled tanks. One day the platoon missed lunch as the platoon leader pushed his men so they would earn more points in the imagined combat. Ron's hunger made him furious. He asked the Sergeant if he and Stubs could go to the personnel carrier and bring back grub for the platoon.

"We'll not eat until nightfall!" the Sergeant barked. "And that's an order."

"He'll pay for this," Ron told Stubs. "He'll pay."

Two weeks later, rehoused in the barracks, Ron was still trying to think of the best way to get even with that smart aleck Sergeant. No other officer had ordered Iceman around so haughtily. Most officers relied on him for loans or dope.

The bunk rooms were always frigid. Wieldflichen had actually been a German army camp in the war, and was not constructed for comfort. Small, dreary rooms were heated by cast iron coal-burning stoves. Ron and Stubs shared a room; just down the hall was the room of the hated Sergeant.

"Rearick," Sergeant Arthurs bellowed one night, "take my coal bucket down to the bin and fill it with coal."

The instant the order was given, Ron had a brainstorm. In his room he had hidden a C.O.-2 cartridge. This seven inch cartridge contained compressed air and was used to instantly inflate military rafts. Ron grabbed the C.O.-2, shoved it down into his own coal bucket making sure it was well hidden, and started down the hall to the Sergeant's room.

"Iceman, you're crazy," Stubbs hissed after him. "It will kill him and we'll be in the brig for life!"

"Here, Sir, take mine for now. I'll fill yours and use it later." Ron meekly handed his bucket to Arthurs. Ron's hatred had been well-concealed for days and the booby-trap was received without suspicion.

Iceman and Stubs walked outside and stood stamping their feet in the cold, waiting for the explosion. The wait was a short one. With deafening force, the cartridge in the stove caught fire and blew out the wall of what had moments before been Sergeant Arthurs' room.

Screaming in confusion, soldiers ran in with fire hoses, medics arrived, and a crowd gathered. Iceman and Stubs calmly strolled to the cafeteria for a cup of coffee.

Miraculously, Sergeant Arthurs was not killed. He had dumped Ron's coal bucket into the stove and then gone to hang his clothes in the metal locker beside his bunk. When the blast hit, the lucky man was behind the open door of that metal locker, and this fact alone saved his life. Metal fragments from the exploding stove embedded themselves in the door. The mattress caught fire and the entire room was demolished. Sergeant Arthurs received second degree burns and was totally deaf for three months.

In the investigation that followed, Ron and Stubs were hauled into court to testify. Ron reported that someone had planted the C.O.-2 cartridge in his bucket in an attempt to kill him or Stubs. "If the Sergeant hadn't ordered us to find him some coal that night," Ron lied, "we would have been dead ducks." The jury believed his testimony.

Sergeant Arthurs knew the truth. From that time on, no one hassled the Iceman, or gave him any cause to be angry. Ron lived like a five-star general for the remainder of his time on base.

ICEMAN

8

The Making of a Hit Man

Ron's comfortable life resembled that of a commanding officer; but this utopia was not to last forever.

Without warning in July of 1965, the Iceman was thrown into Mannheim Military Prison.

Mannheim was a hell hole, rougher than any prison Ron had seen in the States. Twice within three weeks, the entire prison erupted in riots. Even on "calm" days, Ron saw men beaten to death, and others who, in panic, took their own lives. Iceman quickly learned why he had been jailed. The U.S. Army was making a global crackdown on drug-runners in their ranks, and tracked a majority of the dope problem in Germany to PFC Ronald Dave Rearick. Ron could not imagine who had had the nerve to fink on him, but he figured that his 100th birthday would find him rotting in one of the old Nazi cells.

To his amazement, Ron was only in Mannheim for one month before he was summoned to the headquarters office and told that he was being discharged on a "208." The actual term used was "Failure to Adjust."

"Failure to adjust," the recording secretary grimaced. "THAT is the UNDERSTATEMENT of the century!"

Ron figured that when the army intelligence had looked into his activities, they had decided it would be easier to get him off their hands than to attempt to deal with him. By the end of '65, he found himself home in Salt Lake City, a civilian once more. He hadn't even been able to contact his partner Stubs and say good-bye.

"Poor ole Stubs," he thought. "They probably will give him 50 years.

Ron went to work loading trucks for a freight company. It was a great job as far as he was concerned. He was not a likely suspect for any small thefts he might pull on the weekends because he was a steady, dependable worker. There was also a wealth of possessions to be had at the truck loading dock, his for the taking. Huge shipments of televisions, radios, typewriters and other machinery were en route across the country. When one unit of the inventory was missing, it was not discovered for days or weeks.

Ron threw himself 100% into the night life of the area. Iceman was friendly with many hookers and bar maids, as he had always been, but he found he grew more and more lonely. That loneliness waited for him in his apartment like a phantom that surrounded him with gloom at the end of each day. He spent some time with his Mom Opal, now separated from Smiley after years of mental abuse. He sometimes saw his sisters Vi and Sue. Yet his time with them was limited so that he could hide what manner of man he had become.

He found himself thinking about his ex-wife Anna. About little Kathy. "The kid is five years old now," he realized.

His marriage had been a wipe-out. But he was older now. He felt he could really care for a baby. And it would be great to have a little woman home at night with dinner on the table when he walked in the door.

To justify his way of life, Ron had become very good at placing the blame for his actions on everyone else. He had become such a scrapper in school because of the smart-aleck kids who laughed. He had become a thief because the world was full of cheaters anyhow, cheaters like Clarissa. Ron was just gusty enough to work on a bigger scale than most people. He had gotten into black marketing in the service because the Germans appreciated his services, and because the Army was a zoo filled with dumb officers and stupid regulations. He had been such a rotten husband only because Anna had been the wrong kind of wife for him.

It was this mind-set for justifying the past that allowed Ron to step into a second marriage in 1967 with Gwen De La Cruz.

Whereas Anna had been blond, Gwen was brunette. Anna had been lively, tall and outspoken; Gwen was petite and shy. She was a real "homemaker" type who loved to sew and bake. Gwen did not ask too many prying questions, and when it came to Ron's activities, was extremely naive. With Anna, Ron had fathered a girl; with Gwen he fathered Ron, Jr.

Outwardly, the life of Mr. and Mrs. Rearick was similar to that of the majority of the families represented by the men Ron worked with. The lifestyle was merely a temporary cover job, like the snow had been for the countryside of Germany.

Shortly after baby Ronnie was born, Ron's cousin, Jack, moved to Salt Lake City. Jack had been a great buddy since childhood days in the mining towns. He was an Oakie whose father had the best recipe for home-made whiskey in five counties; as soon as Jack arrived, he and Ron built their own still and felt like kids again. Jack was a pilot now, and owned his own Stenson airplane. Ron had been selling dope on a continual basis, but with Jack and the plane, he realized that he could fly into Mexico for the stuff and cut out all of the middle men.

Jack was ready and willing, so in 1966 they began to run what they called the "Tucson Game" across the Arizona border.

They dealt in pot (marijuana) and hash and in pills which were manufactured in underground Mexican laboratories. The pills were what really moved, so they were purchased by the barrel, with 500,000 pills in each one.

One of Ron's best "customers" at the truck loading firm was transferred to San Diego. Whenever the Feds put the heat on the Arizona border, Ron counted on his customer in San Diego to load dope onto a freight truck headed for Salt Lake, and he simply unloaded the package while he was at work. It was a smooth operation; only three men were "in the know."

Ron and Jack would probably have continued their business for years if it had not been for a chance meeting one night in a pool room.

Ron was drinking alone in a classy joint when a hassle started at the end of the bar. A well-dressed businessman had walked in and started yelling obscenities at an older man with silver-gray hair. Ron would not have gotten involved, but as the businessman paced around in a frenzy, he happened to step backwards and sent Ron's whiskey glass crashing to the floor. Ron pounced on him in a rage.

"Listen, Jerk, I can tell you need to learn some manners," Iceman bellowed. "Your fat mouth interrupted my drinking, and now I'm soaked and out of whiskey!" With lightning speed, his fist crashed into the man's jaw and knocked him

out cold. Ron picked up the man's limp body and threw him
out the back door into the alley.

The gray-haired man calmly finished his drink, then
walked over to place a fatherly hand on Ron's shoulder.

"One of my boys was about to take care of that unpleasant
gentleman," he remarked., "but thanks for saving us the
trouble."

The old man left the bar followed by two younger men who
had been drinking across the room. Ron discovered that he
had unknowingly defended Vic Galli, the head of the
organized "family" whose territory covered all of Utah and
Nevada.

Within the week, Galli summoned Ron to the showplace he
called his home. Vic greeted Ron in a mahogany-panelled office decorated with costly antiques and Persian rugs. He offered Ron a place in the organization.

"I've had you checked out, of course, Mr. Rearick. 'Iceman'
that is. Well, Iceman, I'd like to have you join my business."

Ron accepted instantly.

This was a break that he had not even dared to hope for.
He felt that he had, in a sense, "graduated." For years he
had dreamed of a chance to be a real part of the "family" instead of just working with them or for them like a "peon."
But of course a guy couldn't just find them and say, "Hey, I
want to join up!" What a lucky punch he had thrown in that
bar room!

Ron started at $5000 a week, with plenty extra for "ex-
penses" such as his own drug habit. He was employed
basically to do "personal favors" for Vic Galli. Usually this
meant collecting large sums that were overdue.

His first assignment was to convince the head of a hidden
casino in Salt Lake that the Galli family deserved more of
the gambling profits. "Mr. Tecanzo lives alone," Vic in-
formed Ron. "I don't want you to kill him. But once you
break into his house, I don't want you to talk to him, not a
word. He's been talked to already. I just want you to convince him."

"How do you want me to convince him?" Iceman asked.

Vic's expression was emotionless. "Try ripping off his
kneecap."

Ron became one of the family's most successful
employees. "I like my hit men to be convincing instead of
leaving dead stiffs around that are hard to cover," Vic had
told him. And Iceman was convincing. Extremely convincing.

Usually he worked at night, sometimes with a helper

named Joe, slipping into a bedroom and jerking its occu-
pant from a sound sleep into a living nightmare. Most of the
time a few hard blows were all that was needed, along with a
never-to-be-forgotten fear tactic. The scare effect Ron and
Joe used most often was to tie a man in a chair and ram a
shotgun in his mouth.

Ron was also a favorite of The Old Man's because he had a
well-developed instinct for spotting undercover cops. He
never dealt with or even talked to anyone he didn't know.
And he seemed to intuitively know if he was being followed.

One Saturday Ron was shooting pool and spotted a plainclothesman sitting across the room. "That guy is pretty
good," Ron thought. "He's been trailing me off and on for
two days."

Ron went to the bartender and had a drink sent over to the
investigator. "Tell him I'm buying," he grinned.

When the man heard that Ron was buying, he turned as
pale as if he had seen a ghost. He and Rearick were total
strangers; this could only be a signal from the Iceman that
he knew he was being followed. The investigator bolted and
literally ran out of the pool hall.

It was a joke between Ron and Vic Galli for weeks.

Galli gradually began to shift Ron from "muscle" jobs to
"picking up goods" that were coming into the country.
Rearick often traveled to Louisiana to meet boats which had
sailed from Columbia. He made countless trips into Mexico.
He also made frequent flights to Las Vegas with money to be
"washed." By running paper bills through casinos, the
organization could use "clean" bills to invest in legitimate
corporations and businesses.

In January of 1969, Ron and Joe made a standard trip into
Mexico, traveling in a large motor home complete with
fishing reels for Baja and other tourist props. They carried
cash to purchase a large order.

Two men met them at the right place, at the exact time
agreed upon. An abandoned gas station on a lonely stretch
of highway had been the destination. But Ron had been
suspicious from the moment two men pulled in behind the
station in a battered station wagon. He had expected Juan
and Julio; these faces were unfamiliar.

Both men were young, maybe only 20, and sloppily
dressed with shirts stained with grime and perspiration.
Their faces looked tough, but their unsteady steps gave
warning of their nervousness.

"Julio could not come today," one of them said. "I am his
nephew." Neither stranger carried a package which would

contain the merchandise.

"Where's the stuff?" Ron asked.

"We want to see the payment first," came the cool reply.

Ron and Joe stood silent, unmoving. The two strangers could see that their bluff was being called. Only ten feet from the Iceman, the man on the right pulled a handgun and started to fire.

"Get him!" Joe yelled, reaching for his own revolver. But Ron's hand was quicker; his automatic was already aimed. Iceman lurched to one side of the stranger's aim, and as he did he pumped bullets into both men.

Joe and Ron jumped in the motor home and sped toward the U.S. border. Cursing and sweating, they wondered how someone had gotten the details of Julio's operation.

"Vic ain't gonna like this," Joe kept reminding Ron.

Vic Galli was furious.

ICEMAN

9

The Casino King

"But I had no choice!" Ron complained as he faced his boss in Galli's office. "If I hadn't shot them, they'd have blown us away."

"You didn't cause the incident, Iceman, but still I won't be sending you on any out-of-town jobs for a long time." Galli's voice was cold after a long tirade. "You'll stay in Salt Lake and keep a low profile until this hassle dies down."

One of the men Ron had shot turned out to be the nephew of the man who was the kingpin for Galli's dealings in Mexico. Somehow the nephew had uncovered the time and place of Ron's pickup. The Mexican 'godfather' was now steaming, threatening to cut off all business with Galli. But Galli figured out that, in time, the man would cool down and forget about Rearick.

Ron was not to leave the Salt Lake area for months. He felt like a kid who had been 'grounded.'

Galli returned Iceman to the local jobs which required "muscle." Ron once again was making midnight calls, and having 'private consultations' with businessmen. He quickly grew tired of it.

In his entire lifetime, there had been only two occupations which interested Ron. The first he had now accomplished; he was working for the "family." Ron had respected organized crime. He had thought that it was a well-thought-out machine, smoothly operating, secretive in its dealings. He had had the romantic notion that members of a 'family' had some sort of code of honor that assured their loyalty to each other. He had also been certain that the men in the syndicate were smarter than the average punk pulling robberies on the streets.

He had viewed his entry into Galli's business the way an executive would view a career with a prestigious firm. Now, after seeing life on the inside, his romantic notions had crumbled. Instead of organization and efficiency, he had seen sloppiness. Instead of a code of honor, it was 'every man for himself.' Instead of brilliance and cunning, he saw average hoods who often made stupid mistakes. But more than anything, he saw that the operation was often careless with information, letting facts trickle out to federal investigators or to thieves like the two he'd gunned down in Mexico.

He wanted out.

He faced Galli, telling him simply that he was quitting. Galli had never had that happen before. To the surprise of the other men in the office at the time, the big boss gave permission with a nod of his head and a grunt.

Vic knew that Ron was more tight-lipped, and more at odds with the law than most. Iceman would spot any feds who tried to spy on him and he could defend himself if anyone ever applied pressure. Besides, unknown to Rearick, Galli had a lot on his mind at that time.

The "hit man" simply turned and walked away.

All during those months, Ron had continued to live at home with Gwen and baby Ronnie—that is, when he wasn't partying all night or disappearing to do Galli's bidding. Gwen had asked few questions, but she had grown pale and skinny. She knew that there were other women. She could only guess at what her husband did for a living.

One night without warning she confronted him.

"When you leave here tonight, you might as well take all of your clothes with you. I don't want you to ever come back. I don't want you to ever try to see me or Ronnie again." Gwen had squared her shoulders and lifted her chin in attempted bravery, but tears were cascading down her cheeks.

"Maybe she really has loved me," Ron was thinking. "But how could she love me? She doesn't even *know* me."

Without a word, he packed his clothes and walked away.

Besides organized crime, the only other business which ever appealed to Ron was big time gambling. He had dreamed of owning his own casino, of being a casino king.

He decided in July of 1971 that it was time to be his own boss.

Harry Nugent was an acquaintance with years of experience in running a casino. He also had information with which to blackmail the district attorney so that their underground occupation would never be bothered. Ron put up the cash for all of the gaming tables and equipment, and he and Harry became partners. They were co-owners of a casino they named "Vegas North."

Ron had planned on hours of leisure and weeks of vacation with Harry there to run their establishment. During the opening months Ron was always present, 'duded up' in formal attire. Once in a while he had to ruin his nice clothes, such as the night he had to take up a tire chain to drive out three dissatisfied customers. But usually the clients were high-class and dignified.

Yet when it came time for Ron to start enjoying leisure from his profits, the casino king found he was tied to the "Vegas North." He was constantly worried about getting cheated and shortchanged by his dealers or by Harry himself. More than once, Rearick suspected Harry of dipping his hand in the till. But Nugent was the know-how of the business; Ron could not just get rid of him. Iceman had no alternative but to be there to watch his partner all of the time.

Within 5 months, Ron was fed up. "This casino is more of a ball and chain around my neck than marriage was!" he told himself. He wanted out. He asked Harry for a mere $15,000 for his half of the investment.

Ron took the cash and walked away.

"What I need is a vacation. A break from this stupid town," he decided.

With a chick named Rhonda who had inherited a small fortune, Ron lived for a few months like a wealthy playboy. He and Rhonda flew to the coast and learned to sail at Newport Beach. They flew to Acapulco and went deep sea fishing. They returned to the states and spent the summer traveling to the massive rock concerts; through stoned ears they heard Santana, Chuck Berry, and the rest of the superstars.

They went to one big dope party after another. The nights blurred together in his mind; Iceman could barely even remember the name of the town he was in.

They were back in Salt Lake City on the one night of the entire summer that remains clear in Ron's memory. He and Rhonda were using heroin and "coke" in a posh apartment with a dozen acquaintances. Suddenly one of the girls screamed, "Eddy! Eddy! Oh, no—he's overdosed. He's gone."

Ron pushed Eddy's hysterical girlfriend aside and picked the limp, clammy body up in his arms. He carried Eddy to the bathtub and dumped him in, turning on the faucet and filling the tub with water. Then Ron ran to the bedroom and grabbed a big lamp. He plugged the lamp in by the tub, then threw the lamp into the water.

Sparks flew and the lamp exploded and Eddy's body convulsed with the force of the electric shock. An instant after the lamp hit the water, Ron pulled the plug. Eddy lay stiff as a board, but he was breathing.

Iceman had seen dopers shocked back to life several times—usually they were propped in a running shower and didn't receive as much of a jolt as Eddy had. But this place had no shower and the tub had been Eddy's only chance. Ron knew he had saved the kid's life.

He instructed the others to keep Eddy awake, to walk him and give him coffee. Ron went into a back bedroom to calm down and get over the ache in his bones from the part of the current that had gone through his own body.

There was a tiny two-year-old girl lying on a pallet in that room. She was slowly sucking on a bottle, but hearing Ron she turned glazed eyes toward him and tried to stand up. But she couldn't. The baby was drunk.

Ron knew her folks had given her wine in that bottle, and maybe drugs as well, to keep her subdued and quiet while they partied. Ron had seen this many times before, but that night it sickened him. Combined with the shock he had just given Eddy, the sight of the drugged baby was more than he could stand. "This is insane," he groaned. "Only crazy people would live like this."

Ron strode to the front door and, without a word to Rhonda, walked away.

The next morning, Ron realized he was on the verge of going berserk. His insides were about to blow apart and turn him into a raging madman. Before it happened, he knew he had to get away alone. He jumped in his car and drove to Rhonda's secluded mountain cabin.

Later when he would remember the four days he had spent in that mountain cabin, he likened his actions to those of a wounded grizzly bear. Grizzlies are dreadful creatures by nature, but when a grizzly has been badly wounded he becomes an instrument of destruction. It is as if the animal senses he is about to die and is determined to destroy as much as he can in the time he has left. Hunters have tracked wounded grizzlies through miles of broken tree limbs, uprooted saplings and rutted ground, amazed and terrified by the signs of fury the bear has left in the terrain.

It was as if the Iceman knew that he was headed down a path of sure destruction, and since he could not avoid his own destruction, his subconscious mind pushed him to destroy whatever was in his path. He smashed through the cabin's window panes with his bare hands. He ripped the furniture apart, piece by piece. He tore the curtains and bedclothes apart and smashed the dishes. When his tormented body finally collapsed on the floor, there was not one thing in the entire cabin left unharmed.

It was this wounded grizzly bear kind of reaction that caused people to grab a gun and shoot strangers at random, or to drive their car into a crowd of defenseless pedestrians. If he had not sensed the madness before it hit him, there would have been no hope for any human being he was near.

Limp and exhausted, but once more in control of his senses, he left the battered cabin and drove back to Salt Lake City. He stayed in his apartment only long enough to shower and pack his clothes. He would go to Las Vegas, he decided, and gamble and relax until he could come up with a plan. A plan to change his life.

He had tried life as a normal family man, and had walked away in disappointment. He had tried life as part of the "organization," and had walked away in disgust.

But there *had* to be some kind of plan, some sort of change that would put him on easy street. Ron Rearick would *not* end his existence in a "crazy farm" in a padded cell!

It was this buildup of years of lawlessness that brought the man called Iceman to the night in March, 1972 in the Utah desert. It was this buildup of a lifetime of frustration that gave him such anguish when he looked at the million dollars in his possession and knew, "It will not be enough." And it was the climax of years of violence that left him waiting on the highway, wasting priceless getaway moments as he rolled down his car window so he could hear Stubs and the B.A.R. massacre the federal investigators.

ICEMAN

10

The Hanging Judge

"Come on, Stubs! Let them have it!" Ron shouted into the heedless quiet of the Utah desert.

The Iceman leaned his head out of the car window, listening with every fiber in his being for the sound of the Browning Automatic Rifle to explode with violence against the men of the FBI.

"Let them have it, Stubs! I'm waiting!" he screamed once more, and ripped open the shroud of silence around him with a string of profanities. The flightbag with its million dollars lay beside him on the seat, but Ron had known the instant it was in his possession that even this would not bring satisfaction.

"It's not enough," he kept thinking, and a mind twisted by years of violence felt that someone should pay for his frustration. He wanted to hear for himself the sound of Stubs blasting those Feds to kingdom come, even though he knew he was wasting his get away time.

Suddenly the night exploded, not with the expected sound, but with light. Ron and his car and the road were flooded with light and Ron jumped in terror . . . the effect of the light was magnified because it had come without a sound of warning. He knew instantly that the headlights and searchlights were from the car of the Feds.

Iceman floorboarded his Camaro and raced down the two

lane highway. He put every ounce of his will behind the power of his engine. The speedometer rose past sixty, past seventy, past eighty. "If I can just get far enough ahead of them," he schemed, "I can hit the cut-off and make it to the plane." Maybe he would be able to start it and take off even without Stubs, the pilot.

His car sped up and over a small hill. Suddenly he saw that he was headed right into a road block made of three patrol cars. Ron slammed on the brakes and braced himself against the friction of tires burning against cement. The Chevy spun sideways in a cloud of sand and gravel, stopped inches from the barricade. Ron slumped over the wheel, then sat up and raised his hands in surrender. There were enough gun barrels pointed at him to sheer off the top of his car. "Fool!" his mind yelled. "Idiot! You wasted priceless getaway moments for vengeance against the feds."

Angry hands jerked him from his seat, cuffed him, and threw him against the car door to be searched. Four federal investigators got out of the sedan that had chased him.

"Take it easy—I haven't done anything," Ron yelped.

The officer in charge grabbed Ron's shoulder and spun him around. "Then what are you doing out here tonight? And where did you get that bundle of money?"

Iceman's mind flashed back to his days in the army, when he had been able to convince a jury that he had nothing to do with the explosion that almost killed his sergeant. He covered his anger with meekness, and answered the officer like a naive cowpoke.

"I was just headed into Salt Lake, and the oil light in my car came on. So I pulled over beside a dry creek bed and this guy threw something out of the window. He was goin' so fast he didn't even see my car."

"Well, I waited a few minutes, but then I thought I'd best go see what he'd gotten rid of. And, Lordy, I found that United Airlines bag just stuffed with all that money. Must be thousands. Let me tell you, I was afraid. I figured it had been stolen, so I was on my way right now to turn that money in . . ."

"Sure, fella, sure," the lawman interrupted. "Then why did you run from us?"

"I didn't know you were policemen! I saw them lights but I didn't hear no siren. For all I knew, you were crooks come to pick up the money. So I got out of there." Ron lied, looking the man calmly in the eyes.

In the meantime, several policemen had been tearing Ron's car apart, looking for a weapon. "Lt. Neilson," one of the men reported, "We can't find a weapon of any kind."

Investigator Neilson's eyebrows shot up in surprise. Maybe this simpleton was telling the truth. How could a man hijack a million dollars and not be armed?

Ron was even more surprised than the lawmen. Moments before, he had placed his .38 on the seat beside him, right on top of the flight bag. What in the world had happened to it?

Let's take him on in to the courthouse before we question him any more," the FBI man who seemed to be in charge gave direction. "Send two cars back to stake out that creek bed."

The ride to town was not a long one, but it was long enough for Ron to ask himself one question a thousand times. "What in blazes could have happened to Stubs?"

At the courthouse, Ron was read his rights, then questioned for half an hour by the FBI man. He answered smoothly, as if he had nothing to fear. Next he was questioned by the county sheriff, then by another federal investigator.

The scene in that office became ironically comical. Ron was talking to the lawmen as if they were old buddies. They gave him coffee, cigarettes—one even remarked that the airlines would probably have a reward for such an honest citizen. Ron leaned back in his chair, relaxing with his feet up on a desk top. They have no real evidence against me, he thought. I'll keep cool during the questioning, waltz out of here, and be out of the country before morning.

Abruptly, one of the FBI men who had pursued Ron strode into the room from a back office with a computer printout in his hands. He knocked Ron's feet off the desktop and grabbed the cigarette right out of Ron's mouth.

"The joke's up, Rearick," he gruffed. "Your record has caught up with you."

"Book him, Sheriff. Without bail."

The trial began on April 15 in the Superior Court of Salt Lake City. Ronald Rearick was charged with interfering with commerce by threats of violence, conveying information regarding the destruction of an airliner and its passengers, and attempted extortion against United Airlines.

Rearick's two lawyers felt they had a solid case for the defense. No weapon was ever found in Ron's car, neither was there any incriminating evidence from a search of his apartment. (Ron figured the B.A.R. was rusting in the desert.)

The airlines had a tape of Stubs demanding the million dollars, and the prosecutor insisted it was Ron's voice. Voice experts could neither prove nor disprove that the speaker was Rearick.

The jury knew that the money had been recovered in Ron's possession. Ron had no solid alibi. And he had a criminal record a mile long.

After three days of deliberation, the jury found Iceman "guilty as charged."

On May 10, Ron Rearick returned to the courtroom to receive his prison sentence. The night before had been sleepless, as are all the nights before a man receives his sentence, but Ron was more fully awake that morning than he had ever been. He was looking for any chance of escape. He was shackled, hands and feet, but he was desperate.

"They will go hard on you, Ron," his lawyer had told him honestly. "You know that they have been after you for years."

The courtroom was full; the Iceman was only one out of three hijackers who were to be sentenced that day. Besides Ron and his lawyers and the other two felons with their lawyers, there were family members, acquaintances, and a score of reporters. Opal Rearick was there, although Ron had commanded her to stay away. His sister Sue and his latest lady friend, Connie, were also there.

The judge presiding was the Honorable Willis Ritter. Seventy-two year old Ritter was the worst possible man that Ron could have been facing. Known as the "hanging judge," Ritter had, in his years on the Federal bench, built up a reputation for his severity and harsh sentences.

The first man called before the bench was Earl Coleman. As Ron looked at the man, it was clear that he was mentally imbalanced. Coleman had hijacked a jet out of Dallas armed with only a water pistol and a knife. He was captured the minute the plane landed in Utah.

"Earl Coleman, this court has found you guilty of extortion. You are hereby sentenced to 15 years in the federal penitentiary in Springfield, Missouri."

"Do you have anything you wish to say to the court?"

Coleman shrugged his shoulders and stared into space.

"You may take the prisoner away," the Judge ordered.

The next prisoner called to the bench was John McCoy. McCoy was a veteran who had come back from Vietnam with a knowledge of weaponry and survival. Full of hatred and vengeance, McCoy's temper was so explosive that even his parents had called the police one night out of fear. McCoy "cooled down" outwardly, but a few months later had masterminded a scheme against P.S.A. He had bailed out of a plane somewhere near Provo, Utah with over $500,000 in cash.

"John McCoy, this court has found you guilty as charged, of extortion and of holding passengers for ransom. You are hereby sentenced to 45 years in the Leavenworth Federal penitentiary.

"Do you have anything you wish to say to the court?"

McCoy turned to face the observers with a sneer. "The first thing I'm going to do when I get out," he yelled, "is kill my parents and my brother."

There were audible gasps in the courtroom.

"Get that man out of here!" the Judge slammed his gavel in anger against his massive desk.

Ron learned that Coleman hung himself with a bedsheet only six months later. And McCoy was killed in a shootout with police in Chicago after he excaped from prison a year later.

Ron ground his teeth together. He was going to be next, and now Judge Ritter was really stirred up.

"But I wasn't even armed when they caught me. I didn't hold anyone hostage," Ron was thinking, clinging to a last thread of hope for a light sentence.

"Ronald Rearick, approach the bench," the Judge called.

"Rearick, this court has found you guilty as charged of violating the U.S. Penal Code, Section 18. Will the Court's recorder read us this man's record."

The recorder began to read. Iceman's list of criminal offenses went on and on. Fourteen times in jail. Two times in prison. Some of the offenses on that record had been totally forgotten by Ron until that moment. (Of course, the drug dealing and the years of organized crime were not even on that listing.)

Ron glared up at the Judge when the monotone voice finally finished reading. Judge Ritter was smiling. This was *not* a good sign. Ron had heard that the Judge always smiled before pronouncing stiff sentences.

"Rearick, you are hereby sentenced to 25 years at MacNeil Island Penitentiary.

ICEMAN

11

Getting Comfortable

The thoughts of men headed to prison for the first time are as varied as the men themselves. But the thoughts of men who have done time and who know they are headed to the joint again are much the same. These men know that they have to get mentally prepared. Even as he was returned to his cell, Ron began a mental process which he called, "Shaking off any weakness."

In prison, any show of feeling, any show of kindness, would be looked on as a weakness. And men who went in with weaknesses often didn't come out. Weak men who somehow lived through violence from other inmates often cracked up and took their own lives.

In the cell where Ron had been held for several weeks, there was a kid Ron called "Popeye." He was a strange looking, backward sort of young man, skinny and shriveled from drug abuse. Somehow Ron had felt pity for that kid, pity like he used to feel in gradeschool. All the boy owned was a baggy sweatshirt and an old pair of jeans. One day when his girlfriend Connie had come to visit, Ron had instructed her to go buy a suit, shirt and tie for Popeye to have for his trial.

When Ron returned to that cell, the other inmates read the harshness of his sentence on his face. Popeye walked over to put a comforting hand on Ron's shoulder.

"Get away from me, you creep!" Ron yelled, and threw Popeye against the wall.

Ron had mentally left the everyday world behind. His mind was set for prison.

After a three day, cross-country drive, chained hand and foot in a patrol car, Ron found himself facing the navy blue water of the Puget Sound in Washington state. The patrol car was boarding a ferry, and the loudspeaker of the boat announced through burst of static that the first stop was MacNeil Island. Two miles across the saltwater, MacNeil Penitentiary was clearly visible, its massive walls towering above the tallest branches of the fir trees.

"The darn place looks like Alcratraz," commented one of the officers in the front seat.

Ron set his chin, and looked straight ahead.

Arriving at MacNeil, Ron and several other incoming convicts went to the customary "fishtank." They were searched and told to shower, dressed in white coveralls and prison slippers, and introduced to the prison's layout. In his week in the tank, Ron visited the dentist, the doctor, and the psychiatrist, and assigned the task he would perform while in prison.

On the fifth day, he was instructed to go out and find himself a cell, knowing from experience that if he didn't find one quickly on his own, they would assign one. An ex-con knows what kind of cell to look for. If there is no room in a cell with someone you already know, you look for one that seems "clean" and "quiet."

A first-timer could end up in a cell with a group of finks. Or fairies. Or a group that the other men in the prison were after. But Ron knew how to tell the "cons" (the men who knew *how* to do time) from the "inmates." The cons were neatly dressed, their bunks were tidy and usually had newer blankets; they clearly had access to the better supplies of the prison and were finding ways to get "comfortable."

Ron picked a cell with a Utah native he knew as Jess. Besides Jess, there were 6 other men in the 12' by 12' room. Two bunk beds stood end-to-end against each wall, and between the beds was a battered table. Opposite the barred entrance to the cell was a three-foot high bookcase, and behind that was the toilet and the sink. Under each bunk there were footlockers for the men's underwear and a few belongings.

"Guess I'll sleep up there." Ron jerked his thumb to an empty upper bunk.

"Yep," said the man lying on the bunk beneath it.

On the way up, Ron purposely stepped on the chest of that man.

"Watch it!" the guy yelped, cursing Iceman.

Ron didn't utter a sound, but on the way down he stepped firmly on the man's neck. One look into Ron's face told the smaller man that Ron was no one to mess with.

"Guess you can have the lower bunk," he said, and then silently moved to the higher berth.

There were 3700 men in MacNeil Prison, most of them divided into these eight-man-cells. The inmates had committed a myriad of different crimes, and there were few small-time offenders. Two of the others in Ron's cell were doing 75-year sentences. One had a ninety-year-term. One had been sentenced for three hundred years.

Ron met men in the prison yard who were serving 600 year sentences. Many of the trusties he talked to had been in prison since the thirties. Ron even ran into foreigners who were convicted spies and an Eskimo who was serving time for cannibalism.

For a few weeks, Ron just surveyed the place before he decided to get in on any action. His assigned work was as a cook in the hospital building. He thought of that as a real break; he had a chance to eat a little better, and he was close enough to the medical storerooms to rip off a needle or some pills. (He was not "hard up." Friends were already providing him with hash and pot.)

The Iceman became friendly with a medical trustie named Freddy, a Jewish man who had been trained as a medic in Korea. It was clear that Freddy was selling the pills to which he had access. He graciously offered to let Ron in on the profits if Ron would serve as his muscle man in collecting the dues. Ron stifled a laugh and pretended to be honored at the offer, but for days simply watched Freddy closely. One afternoon Ron was standing inconspicuously behind a door when Freddy tipped a chair over, pryed off the rubber tip of a chair leg, and inserted a wad of bills in the hollow metal tube.

So that's where he keeps his business! Ron thought. The next day when Freddy was not on duty, it was a simple matter to search the chair legs in that room. Ron made off with $400 in cash and 30 "upper" capsules. He cut slits in a thick newspaper and inserted the pills, then taped in the money and folded the paper so that even if it was unrolled it would look normal. His precautions were important—on the way back to his cell he was checked by a hall guard in one of the common "random searches."

The $400 was used to purchase a pound of marijuana from the outside through a guard who had been blackmailed. Ron and his cellmates broke the pot down, kept plenty for themselves, and still doubled their money. From then on, Ron had the assets to roll big time and take over the drug running in his area of the prison.

Professional cons have many ways to get drugs into the "joint." Ron usually chose to find a young inmate with no drug record, and "convince" him to bring in deliveries. A woman from the outside would prepare the delivery by placing thumbnail-sized amounts of coke or heroin inside a deflated balloon and securing the balloon with a tight knot. She would hold the balloon in her mouth and pass it to the young inmate when she kissed him during a visit. During one visit, the "pick-up" man would swallow several balloons, return to his cell and take a large dose of laxative. Then the drugs would be removed from the balloon holders and distributed by Iceman and his men.

Rearick's business was lucrative. Many of the men in the prison relied on dope to get "comfortable"—to be able to stay sane. And the more comfortable his buyers got, the more Ron was comfortable.

Iceman experienced only a few days inside the walls that threatened to undo his mental control. One of those days was close to Christmas in 1973.

All of the men in MacNeil had grown more resentful of confinement with the approach of the holidays. Racial tension had grown worse. One-on-one brawls were more frequent. One dinner hour, as Ron ate tasteless food at a cafeteria table, the inner anger of all of the prisoners exploded in a single act of violence.

A massive hulk of a Chinaman had used a jagged bit of metal to form an ugly homemade knife. For reasons known only to himself, he walked down the aisle of tables and stopped by the black man who ate at the table across from Rearick. Without warning, the Chinaman plunged the jagged knife into the black inmate's throat. As the attacker walked out of the lunchroom, his victim fell to the floor gasping, and in seconds lay dead.

Guards descended on the cafeteria. Every prisoner in the room was questioned, and re-questioned. Every prisoner in the room, including Ron, said that he had not seen a thing.

Ron usually used heroin every day. At parties, he had been known to take five snorts of "big H." That night, he could not remember how much heroin he had snorted or how many pills he swallowed.

It was a few days before Ron began to "maintain" once more. He somehow held on to his comfort zone. That is, until he met The Old Man.

ICEMAN

12

The Melting

The Old Man cornered Ron one afternoon in the prison yard.

The MacNeil Prison yard was a level area two football fields in length, surrounded by a high chain-link and barb wire fence. Three ominous gun towers loomed over this recreational rectangle. The yard included a baseball diamond, a track which also served as a football field, handball courts and a grassy area that had been converted into a miniature golf course. But for Ron, the important part of the yard was a wooden platform known as the "iron pile" where the inmates lifted weights. Iceman had just made a drug delivery to the shed where sports equipment was stored and was headed for the iron pile when the Old Man called him by name.

"Ron," he said, "I have something to tell you."

Rearick turned questioning eyes to the stranger. In the joint, men who don't know each other are very cautious about becoming involved in conversation. Yet Ron relaxed his stance when he saw that the speaker was elderly and white haired, one of those cons who had becomed a permanent fixture at the prison. Tall and slender, his shoulders were bent but he held his chin high. The stranger's demeanor demanded respect. His weather-beaten face was deeply crossed with lines that said that he had seen everything in life that there was to see.

Ron did not ask his name. His eyes were caught by the stranger's piercing eyes.

"I have been in the joint since 1937," the Old Man stated simply. "I can tell that you are a smart man. We've got the best of everything in here. The best safecrackers. The best forgers. They're all here, aren't they?"

"Yeah," Iceman agreed, "MacNeil has some of the best."

"But Ron, if you want to do some learning about peace, there's only one place to learn. You have to look in this book."

He held out a black book that Ron recognized as a Bible.

"Take it, boy." His voice was soft, yet firm. "You can look in it and learn about peace. You can look in it and get ahold of Jesus."

Ron received the gift that was extended. Without another word, the Old Man turned and walked away.

Ron took the book back to his cell and put it under his mattress. A few days later, while the other men lay on their bunks reading the day's mail, he opened the small book and tried to read a few verses. He looked at a few in Psalms, a few Proverbs. He turned to the beginning and read a few "begats." It was rough going with only a third-grade reading level. He got mad and put the book away.

At night when he lay in his bed he could feel it there. He could feel it right through his mattress—or was he just imagining that? One morning he tried once more to read it, but began to curse in frustration. He threw the book across the cell, but decided he'd better pick it up before the others came back and found it.

When he bent down to pick the book up, it lay opened to the sixth chapter of Isaiah. His eyes fell on verse eight:

"And I heard the voice of the Lord saying, Whom shall I send, and who will go for us? Then said I, Here am I, send me."

Ron's eyes traced the words in that verse several times. If he was understanding it right, this was a verse about a man and God actually talking to each other. He placed the Bible back under his mattress, but the verse ran through his head all day.

Was there a possibility, even the slightest chance, that a man could talk to God and that God would talk to a man?

Ron tried to go on with his life as usual, but this idea haunted him. He had never been sure that he believed in God, but now it began to seem as if Someone was following him, trying to get through to him.

"Can Ron Rearick and the Lord talk to each other?" The

question burned in his mind.

"Stop it! Leave me alone!" he said aloud one afternoon in the sunshine of the yard, and then wondered why he had said it. He was standing far away from any other man.

Finally in desperation, he reminded himself that he was a man with courage, a man who would try anything, at least once. He determined to try an experiment that very night.

"Lights out" came at 10:30 p.m., but often the prisoners didn't fall asleep for hours. Sleep is a precious commodity for a man behind bars. During the day he can keep pretty busy, but at night when a man lies alone on his bunk and the past and the future close in on him, he is faced with reality as it really is. For Ron and many others, this is the reason drugs are a necessity in prison; drugs put a troubled mind to sleep.

Iceman waited. He waited for hours, even after all movement in the cell block had ceased. It must have been three o'clock in the morning when he slipped from under his blanket and knelt on the cold cement by the cell door.

He took hold of the black iron bars and bowed his head. Light was streaming in from the hallway, so he closed his eyes.

"God," he whispered quietly so that the night guard would not hear him, "I was wondering if You might listen to me."

He held his breath. He listened. In the entire cell block, not a sound could be heard. In his whole life Ron could not remember a moment so quiet, so still.

"God," he continued, "If You hear me, I was hoping that you might do something with my life."

In an instant, Ron was aware that something was happening, right there in his prison cell. A Presence had entered his cell. He felt that Presence in every fiber of his being. Not just a Presence, he recognized, but a Person. The Lord had entered that cell.

Ron could not have put into words what was happening. There was no sound of thunder, no earthquake. He was not zapped by lightening, nor did his bed catch on fire. Yet Ron was shaken to the core with the certainty that God was meeting him there.

Ron began to weep. He tried to stifle his sobs, but the Person in that cell had reached down inside of him and was turning him inside out. He felt compelled to confess his sins. He began to ask the Lord for forgiveness, mentioning all the crimes of the past, all the sinful actions, all the hatred and bitterness. It was as if years of sludge and debris were being ripped out of his inner man. Ron talked to the Lord for hours; miraculously no one in the cell stirred. Ron prayed and wept quietly, but something cataclysmic, something earthshaking, was happening inside.

Finally, Ron stood up and slipped back into bed. He was overwhelmed by a sense of calm, a sense of well-being. He closed his eyes in thankfulness and slept like a baby.

The next morning this man called Iceman experienced something even more unexpected. The moment he opened his eyes, he knew that the Presence had not left him!

He did not say a word to anyone about what was happening to him. He looked for the Old Man for days, but could not find him. Someone said that several older men had been transferred to Leavenworth. Finally, Ron gave up the search. He never even knew the Old Man's name.

No one had ever talked to Ron Rearick about Jesus before. He had never been in a church service in his entire life. He knew that someone called Jesus had been born at Christmas and died at Easter—that was about it. The words "Christ" and "God" were only used for swearing. And religion was only a crutch for weaklings.

Now this Jesus, this Messiah, was undeniably real and was invading his life.

Ron hadn't the slightest idea of what to do next. He did not often open his Bible because he could barely comprehend the meaning of the letters which were printed on the pages. He did not stop smoking or drinking or taking dope. For some reason, though, he no longer wanted to sell drugs to others, so he only took it when it was provided by friends.

There was nothing different about his life, yet somehow everything seemed different. No matter how hard he tried, Ron could not figure out what was going on.

One day a few weeks later, Ron looked at his face in the mirror above the sink in his cell. Ron had always hated to look at his own image. It was not the scars on his face or the damage that fighting had done to his nose. The fact was that for years he had not been able to look back at the reflection of his own eyes. Yet that day in MacNeil Island Federal Penitentiary, Ron was surprised to learn that he could now look at his own reflection without flinching.

The man in that mirror, especially the eyes of the man in the mirror, looked somehow changed, somehow different. Ron's face seemed the same—yet not the same. He stood there staring at himself in amazement.

He could not understand it.

An indefinable flame had been kindled in his heart. From the inside out, the Iceman was beginning to melt.

ICEMAN

13

A Unique Technique

"Get ready to go, Rearick. We're sending you back to Salt Lake City."

"Salt Lake?" Ron stood in the Warden's office, staring at the man in confusion. "Why?"

"I have no idea," the Warden replied. "All I know is that Judge Ritter is calling you back to court."

During the long ride back to Salt Lake City, Ron sat silently in the patrol car trying to think of a possible explanation. Had Stubs turned up so that Ron was needed to testify against him? Had the federal agents traced Ron's connections with the Galli family's drug dealings? (The prison grapevine is dependable; Rearick had heard that the feds had finally put old Vic Galli behind bars, pinning him on a tax evasion charge.) Ron had phoned his Salt Lake lawyers as soon as the Warden had given him the news, but they knew nothing, not even that he had been summoned back.

"This is highly unusual," Mr. Van Huse had told him, "unless they have decided to add to your sentence because of your other crimes."

The police car had just crossed the Utah border when a news item on the radio exploded in Ron's mind:

"...This morning the honorable Judge Willis Ritter suffered a heart attack in his Salt Lake City home. Judge Ritter has served on the Federal Board for 21 years. He is listed in critical condition at the University Hospital . . ."

Judge Ritter? A heart attack?

When Ritter had sentenced McCoy that day two years ago, McCoy had threatened to kill his own parents. When Ritter had sentenced Ron, the Iceman did not say a word. But he had planned to murder someone, too, if ever he escaped and got a chance. He had planned to kill Judge Ritter, that "hanging judge" who had smiled when he had sentenced Ron to 25 years.

Yet after hearing the news bulletin, Ron wasn't even thinking how this turn of events might affect him. He found himself realizing that the old man was probably on the edge of eternity without the knowledge that there was a God. The judge was *not* a popular man. Probably no one had ever prayed for him. That night when Ron lay on a cot in Salt Lake City jail, he said a prayer for Judge Ritter. Somehow his deep hatred for the man was all gone.

If Ron had taken time to realize the irony of the situation, he would have been overwhelmed by how much he was changing inside. Three years ago, Ron had stayed in this very cell, dreaming of killing the man who had pronounced his sentence. Now, Judge Ritter became the first person besides himself that Ron ever prayed for!

Several weeks went by. No one knew what to do with Ron. Rearick learned that the Judge *was* recovering, but was amazed when he heard that the Judge had resumed some of his courtroom responsibilities.

Ron Rearick once again stood before the bench of the "hanging judge."

The Judge looked frail, shrunken. He gazed down at Ron and in a weakened voice asked the court recorder, "What is this man doing in my courtroom?"

"I don't know, Your Honor," the man replied.

"What is this man doing back in my courtroom?" This time the question was directed to Ron's lawyers.

"We don't know, Your Honor," Mr. Van Huse replied.

"No, you don't know," the Judge remarked strangely. "No one knows why he's here except me."

He turned to look down at Ron. "I have called you back to court for one reason. One night several months ago I just found it in my heart to call you back here, and to give you a pardon."

Two hours later, Ron Rearick was on the streets of Salt Lake City, a *free man.* He was stunned. His legs were so shaky that he could barely walk. "Pardoned," he kept repeating, "Pardoned by the hanging judge."

It was beyond comprehension.

It was miraculous.

The same God who had met him in a prison cell had now swung the prison doors open wide.

Opal Rearick still lived in the city. Ron went to live in her home for a while, and he was able to get hired back at the Freight Company. His family, his old friends, his fellow workers all laughingly called his return a miracle. They tossed the word "miracle" around lightly. But Ron never laughed when he said the word.

He had no idea of what was going on. He could not imagine what might happen next. All he knew was that something was going on between Ronald Dave Rearick and God Almighty.

In those days after his release, Ron barely prayed, and didn't ask God for anything; he was afraid that God would do it!

The ex-con knew absolutely nothing about how to grow spiritually. In the days he worked loading the trucks, and in the nights he drank whiskey and smoked dope, usually with just a few friends. For some reason that he couldn't put his finger on, he no longer enjoyed big drug parties. He didn't even consider going to a church—he felt he had to "get himself together" before he could be seen in such a holy place.

One Friday night, though, Ron decided to go to a big bash in East Salt Lake. He had decided that it was high time for him to give God the credit for touching him in prison and for getting him released. "I got to pay Him back somehow," he was thinking. "And what better place to talk about God than a dope party?"

Most of the group was stoned by the time Ron arrived. He found an old acquaintance sitting alone on the sofa and cornered him.

"Hey, Brad," Ron said loudly, just inches from the man's face, "I want you to know that it was God Almighty that got me out of prison."

Brad looked back at Ron without response.

"I called on God, Brad. You need to call on Him, too."

Brad did not speak. His eyes were dazed, so Ron decided to go "witness" to someone else. An hour later, Ron was entering the kitchen when he overheard Brad talking to the host of the party.

"What new trip is the Iceman on?" Brad asked. "Can you imagine *him* telling me to call on God?"

"Yep, Ron's gone and got religion," the host answered.

"But just give him a hit of heroin or coke, and he'll shut up."

That statement hit Ron like a slap in the face. Was this what others thought of his newfound faith in the Lord? That it could be "bought" for the bribery of a bit of dope? Instantly sober, Rearick slipped out the back door and headed home.

In the living room of the apartment he had rented, Ron fell on his face on the floor and for the second time in his life, cried out to God. This time he did not have to pray quietly; his thoughts and feelings burst out of him in a torrent of anguish.

"Help me Lord! I want to tell people about You. I owe You at least that much. But they won't listen cause they think drugs are my real God. You know how it is with me and the dope. I've tried to quit before, but I can't do it if You don't take away the need for them. Oh, Jesus, have mercy on me!"

In the midst of his tearful praying, Ron sensed God speaking to Him once again. Ron realized that the Lord had not touched him so he could "pay the Lord back," but rather because He loved Ron. And it was the power of God's love that would take away his drug habit.

Ron was overwhelmed with how God's love had protected him. Soon after Rearick was in prison, his "hit-man" partner, Joe, had been shot and killed while asleep in his wife's arms. The same month that Galli was sent to prison, Galli's three brothers were gunned down in Chicago. And after his return to Salt Lake City, Ron had discovered that God had graciously kept him from being an actual murderer: the two men he had shot at close range in Mexico had not died!

Still, Ron had never imagined a power so great that it could break the addiction that had bound him for 12 years. Ron's system craved larger doses of dope than were taken by anyone else he knew. He had never heard of "The Cross And The Switchblade" or any testimony of that nature, and he wasn't sure if anyone had ever dared to ask God for deliverance from this bondage.

But when Ron stood up from that night of prayer, he was totally free from the heavy chains of addiction. He never again felt the desire to smoke pot or drop acid or shoot heroin. He did not go through emotional upheaval. He did not experience pain or tremors or other withdrawal symptoms.

In the late sixties, a revival had begun in California which had sent many Jesus People into the towns across America to share their faith in the Lord. There were now Jesus People in Salt Lake City, especially in an area known as Liberty

Park. One day in the park's green oasis, Ron noticed a couple of young men handing out tracts.

"That's it!" Ron exclaimed. "That's how I can witness!" Thrilled by the fact that he was now "clean" from drugs, Ron had been yearning to discover just how he could become involved in "God's business." He found the address of a Christian supply store in a phone book, and went right over to purchase his own supply of leaflets.

Back in the park, he stationed himself on a corner and began to hand them out. It is very difficult to refuse a tract from a man who looks like Ron Rearick, and none of the pamphlets were turned down. By afternoon, Ron had to return to the bookstore for more!

The next day, Sunday, Ron headed to the park once again. This time he not only gave out the papers—he began to watch how the people reacted after they had received them.

Some walked away slowly, scanning the words on the leaflets. Some tucked them into pockets or purses. But others, in fact many others, just tossed the tracts aside once they were a few yards away.

Ron began to get really hot. What kind of respect was that, to throw away a message about God's love? Especially when a man had gone and bought that message for you out of his own paycheck?

Just then a college student accepted a tract, but then crumpled it and tossed it aside just a few yards from Ron. That was a big mistake.

Ron grabbed the kid by the collar. "Hey, fella. Is that all a message from God means to you?" he yelled.

The young man's eyes were wide with shock. Still, he attempted to make a strong stand.

"I do not want to hear about God. I do not believe in Him."

"Oh, really?" Ron asked sarcastically. Still holding the boy's collar, he shook him violently. "Well, it just so happens that there is a God, and He deserves your respect."

"I want you to pray right now and ask Jesus to come into your life," Ron commanded.

The boy was frowning. Ron lifted the kid off the ground with one hand and gave him a stinging slap with the other. "I said, 'Ask Jesus into your heart'!"

Knowing that this Jesus Freak was a real nut, the young man began to obey. Ron the evangelist turned him loose and sent him on his way.

Ron felt extremely high that night. It had taken him a while, but he had finally made his first convert!

ICEMAN

14

The Difference

"Who *is* that man?"

The young pastor was speaking to his assisting minister in a whisper, not turning his head or moving his lips, but keeping concerned eyes on the burly individual who was giving a boisterous testimony.

"I don't know," the assistant answered, "I'm sure he's never visited the church before."

It was the Wednesday night prayer and praise service, and after a time of worship, Pastor Ted Montana was leading the congregation of New Hope Chapel in open sharing. A teenage boy had stood first, telling that he was becoming bolder in his stance as a Christian. "The Holy Spirit has even been helping me witness to friends at school who are members of different cults," he concluded.

A young housewife had shared next, continuing that theme. "Cult members are after converts because they are actually working for their salvation. They pull people into organizations which don't even teach that Jesus is Savior and Lord. Lately I've been more zealous to share my faith because if we don't get to people who are spiritually hungry, the cults will."

The large man who introduced himself as Ron had stood next, and it was the content of his sharing, more than even his tough appearance and manners, which concerned the pastor.

"I don't understand you people." Ron had boomed. "I just don't understand you! If you know, like I do, that those people are teaching the wrong things, then why don't you do something about it? Why let them get away with it?"

"I've been looking at stories in the Old Testament, and gosh, did those Israelites know how to take care of trouble! Don't you remember the story of Jericho, how the walls tumbled down and the enemy was destroyed?"

"God touched my life while I was in prison. Then He got me released and took me off all the dope I was on. Now I want to do some things for Him. Now I am really good with explosives—guess I know as much as any man alive. With a couple of you to help, we could go and wire that big place down the street and blow it sky high! We'd make sure it was empty first. By morning we'll have won a *real* battle for the Lord!"

Ron was obviously serious, and the people seated around him swallowed hard and looked to their pastor for direction. Rev. Montana was amazed by the man's words, but he was looking at the man with a genuine smile. The ex-con was a tough individual, but the pastor sensed the sincerity of Ron's heart and felt a Spirit-given love for him.

"Ron, we rejoice with you in all God is doing in your life. And we're really glad you can be with us tonight. I share your concern for people caught in the cults. But, Brother, when Jesus died on the cross and rose again, we stepped into the era of the New Testament. Jesus came to extend forgiveness and grace. Until He returns again, we are in an Age of Grace. We are to leave judgment in His hands; His second coming won't be in humility, but in power. Right now, Ron, Jesus is patiently extending grace and forgiveness. He asks us to extend that grace and forgiveness in everything we do."

"If you'd like to talk more about this, I'd love to have you join me in my office for coffee after the service."

Ron returned the minister's smile and nodded his acceptance. He liked the looks of Pastor Ted—athletic, and obviously not a wimp or a weakling—and he liked being treated like a friend.

Before Ron entered his office that night, Ted Montana had a chance to phone Rev. Paul Phillips who pastored a Baptist Church nearby. Ted had overheard Ron saying that he often attended Pastor Phillips' services.

"Yes, Ron Rearick is quite a character," Rev. Phillips admitted. "He's got a lot of rough edges, but he's already come a long way in these last few months. At least when he shares a testimony now he leaves out most of the dirty words. He's stopped cussing at any church folks who accidentally park in "his" parking space. A while back he even asked me to let him share a little sermon on Sunday night."

"Oh, really? How did he do?"

"Well, he gave a three-minute talk on 'Noah and the Whale'. . . does that answer your question?"

Montana and Phillips both laughed loudly. "Do you think I should talk to him a little more tonight, to cool his "ministry" of explosives?" Ted asked.

"Oh, yes!" Pastor Phillips' tone was urgent. "If you don't, he just might try it!!!"

A few weeks after he had started handing out tracts, Ron had decided he should start going to church. He had chosen a small group of believers near his apartment and had thrown himself into Christianity with his usual 100% whole-hearted determination.

The phrase "a bull in a china closet" describes perfectly his entrance into Christian circles. The Church seemed like a maze to Ron—a confusing, bewildering maze. He did not speak their language—words like "redemption" and "conviction" were meaningless—and they certainly didn't speak *his* language. He had no idea whatsoever which actions were accepted and which were not.

Pastor Phillips was a distinguished-looking man in his 60's. He was kind and filled with wisdom. He knew that in order to grow Ron needed time and much teaching. The pastor had even paid Ron's tuition for nightly classes in a local Bible institute. Ron had entered the institute with enthusiasm. After all, several church members had already told Ron he was headed for a ministry. "This institute must be the doorway," he thought.

(One woman had even told him that testimonies like his were needed in the "Bible Belt." Ashamed to ask what she meant, Ron had pictured himself preaching to workers in a factory with long conveyor belts down which were rolling hundreds of newly-printed Bibles.)

Ron's enrollment in the Institute only lasted two weeks. He sat through lectures unable to read the textbooks and unable to find verses in his Bible. Pastor Phillips had not realized the ex-con could barely read. One night the instructor told the students to go home and read over their notes, and Ron knew he was done for; he couldn't even write down the notes that he was supposed to take home and study.

When Ron thought of "God's business," he could come up with only one other category of ministry besides preaching the Bible. He had seen it in the church and on Christian TV shows—that ministry was singing.

Ronald Rearick, ex-dope pusher, ex-hit man, ex-hijacker, found the best voice instructor in Salt Lake City and hired her to teach him to sing. He paid Mrs. Carson $30 an hour, twice a week, to work with his foghorn of a voice.

After weeks of bellowing ridiculous "la la la la las," Ron sounded the same—hopelessly monotone. Mrs. Carson, fearful of speaking the whole truth, finally told him, "I just don't feel I can continue to charge you the normal rate, Mr. Rearick. But I will certainly be glad to instruct you free of charge."

It was an awful blow. His singing career was over.

Ron felt like such a failure. "I flunked out of Bible and I flunked out of singing." In reality, Ron thought he was actually flunking out of Christianity. How could a guy be a Christian if he couldn't read or write or sing?

Ron made the rounds of almost every home Bible study and every Christian happening in the area. Members of groups such as businessmen's fellowships became well acquainted with his unique personality. He brought a certain amount of tension to every meeting he entered—no one ever knew what he might do or say.

Ron made mistakes, but he also saw other Christians "blowing it." He walked into church circles with eyes that had the clear discernment of childlike faith. Once, in a group claiming financial prosperity, Ron spoke up and asked how they could have faith for possessions and yet not enough faith to quit habits like smoking. After his question, the room grew uncomfortably quiet.

Another time, a man wanting to start a church in his home asked Ron to be one of his group's "elders." *"Elder?"* Ron retorted. "Isn't that someone who's kind of an old-timer in the faith? Why, I'm just a beginner. How do you know I wouldn't lead your people down a wrong path? I'd be more careful about handing out titles and picking elders if I was you."

Yes, there were awkward, painful moments. Ron's attempts to fit into the machinery of church life would never have worked if, flowing between the parts of that machinery, there had not been plenty of the *anointing oil of love.*

His fellow Christians loved him. They really did. He felt them receiving him and accepting him just as he was. He felt them being patient, although he was very impatient with himself. He was "hugged-on" and invited over for dinners. When he brought street bums and gaudy women to church and forced them to sit beside him in the front row, he saw them welcomed in spite of their rudeness. He was prayed for continually. He was encouraged by several different dedicated pastors, men of God from all backgrounds and all denominations.

He was especially aware of this love from the body of Christ on the last day that he ever tried his unique method of handing out tracts in Liberty Park.

It had been months since he had purchased a handful of tracts, and it was several weeks after Ted Montana talked to him about "leaving judgment in God's hands." One Saturday morning Ron was feeling especially useless to the kingdom of God remembering that he was a failure as a Bible scholar *and* a failure in singing. He decided once more to try street witnessing, telling himself that now he knew some answers in case anyone tried to argue.

The summer sun was already scorching the sidewalk when Ron arrived at his usual corner in Liberty Park. By 11:00 a.m. the temperature was 90 degrees. By noon it was nearing 100. Ron was feeling pretty proud of himself. Even in the tormenting heat, he had not lost his temper even once or gone after an individual to hit him or kick him.

Then Ron was confronted with the totally unexpected. A ridiculous character with a shaved head and an orange sheet for clothing stationed himself on the same corner. The crazy dude started hopping up and down and banging on a tambourine and chanting mumbo-jumbo!

"Beat it, fella . . . if you *are* a fella!" Ron warned him. "This is *my* corner."

The orange bedsheet kept hopping, the bells kept jingling, and the chant grew louder.

"Listen, clown! I told you to beat it!"

Words weren't working. Ron decided to try another approach. His rugged fist held a tract in the face of the "Krishna." "I want you to take this somewhere and *read it!*" Ron commanded. "It will tell you about Jesus."

The kid stopped dancing and looked at Ron with spacey eyes. "Do you eat meat or fish or eggs?" he asked.

"Yeah . . . why in the world are you asking?"

"If you eat meat or fish or eggs, you are not truly religious," the "Krishna" replied.

That did it. Ron had no answers for an idea as crazy as that. He was baffled, and he was *furious*. He sprang forward and belted the guy, sending him sprawling and ripping the orange robe in half. "So you don't want to hear about Jesus, huh?" Ron yelled. "Well we'll just see if you can change your mind . . ."

Ron lifted him from the ground and was getting ready to punch him again when a hand from behind clutched Ron's shoulder and a man's voice said, "Stop it!"

Ron wheeled to face a long-haired young man, skinny and a head shorter than himself. He held a Bible in one hand and shook the other hand in Ron's face in anger.

"Stop it!" he repeated. "This is *not* of the Lord. Jesus doesn't want you to go around punching people out in His name!"

Out of the corner of his eye, Ron could see that an orange sheet was crawling away to safety. He was about to turn what remained of his anger on this "shrimp" with long hair that had the nerve to shake his finger in Ron's face. Then he realized that he owed this new brother some respect. The other Jesus People in the park had always hid behind trees or slipped quietly away whenever Ron had showed up. He had known that they were afraid of him; this man was not afraid.

"My name's Ben." Ben grabbed Ron's right hand and shook it firmly in greeting. "Let's go get a Coke and talk about the Lord."

The conversation Ron had with Ben over two cold Cokes and a mound of french fries was not a long one, but it was life-changing for Ron. Ben was able to explain that a forced confession of Christ was not a real confession at all—that Romans tells us that faith must come from the heart. Ron admitted that he had worried about whether or not his "conversions" in the park had had any effect at all on those individuals.

"Oh, they probably had some long-lasting cuts and bruises," Ben grinned.

"But how can I keep from losing my temper when someone will show no respect to Jesus?" Ron asked in frustration.

"Brother, what you need in your life is the power of the Holy Spirit! You have entered a new kingdom, but you are still trying to win your battles with the strength of your flesh. Spiritual battles, such as seeing people born again, call for spiritual strength."

"A man called Pastor Ted told me something like that once when we were talking in his office."

"The Bible Study I go to is in the home of a member of his congregation! Why don't you meet with us this Thursday night? We're studying the work of the Spirit, and we always take time to pray for each other."

That Thursday night, Ron did as Ben had suggested. When he arrived, the front door of the small, tidy home was open wide, and a large note on the screen door said "Come On In." Ron did so, and for a moment thought he had made a big mistake.

There were men and women in the kitchen, living room and dining area, and they were all praying. Out loud! Many had both hands lifted high, but others knelt with bowed heads. The prayers were fervent and boisterous, and Ron felt pretty edgy.

"I'll sit in the corner beside that big table lamp," he thought." That way if anyone gets too funny, I can grab the lamp and bash 'em."

As the meeting went on, Ron forgot all about the lamp and became earnestly interested in what these people had to say. After the prayer time there was a time of sharing, then of study, then of singing. Ron may have flunked out of voice lessons, but he found he could do a great job of clapping with their fast choruses.

In closing, the leader asked if there was anyone there who desired the Holy Spirit's moving in his life and would like "the laying on of hands." ("Ah," Ron thought, "so there's a different way to lay hands on someone than the way I've been doing!")

Two people knelt on the living room floor, the prayer group encircling them. Ron slipped to the floor and knelt beside them.

As he closed his eyes, several men put their hands on his head and shoulders. They began to pray. Ron did not hear a word that was said; he was suddenly enveloped with an over- whelming presence of the Lord. Without effort, prayer and praise began to pour from his mouth. He felt as if a river were rushing through him, or as if an artesian well inside of him was released that was splashing over to the outside.

Later they told him that he had knelt and prayed in that same position for over an hour. To Ron it seemed like only a moment. Finally his heart was still. He lifted his head and opened his eyes.

There, directly in front of him, a woman sat on the sofa with her eyes still closed in prayer. She was an attractive woman, petite with blond hair in a curly style which fell to her shoulders. What Ron really noticed, though, was the ra- diance on her face.

The instant that he saw her, something deep in his heart whispered, "There is your helpmate."

Ron was so startled that he stood up and hurried out the door while the prayer group spent time in fellowship.

He felt so clean inside, washed and changed by that river of the Lord's Spirit. His mind was clear, his thoughts sharp, his body so *alive*. Driving home, he rolled down the car windows and the night air blowing on his face felt like the night air had felt when he was a very little boy.

God had worked mighty changes in Ron's soul that night. He was mighty certain of it. And to think that he might also have met the woman he was to marry. . .God was giving more blessing than Ron knew how to contain. Ron started to laugh loudly. He laughed and laughed, he could not stop laughing until he reached his apartment.

Ron had been asking God for a strong Christian wife, a "helpmate" as he had heard in church. He was so tired of the women he knew and the ones he had been dating. He had marched at least half a dozen former lady friends to church with him, with no results at all. Their hearts were not tender toward the Lord. Some of them even admitted they had heard the Gospel before and just "weren't ready."

Ron had been growing impatient. After all, this prayer for a good Christian wife had continued for over six months. None of his other requests had taken nearly that long!

He knew that now, finally, he could be the right kind of husband. He knew that now he could commit himself to one woman and *love* her, because Jesus was making him able to love.

Now he knew who his helpmate was going to be! He could barely control his excitement.

He knew he *had* to be patient a little while longer. After all, he didn't want to rush in and scare her. He couldn't just walk up to her the next morning and say, "You're supposed to marry me!" He would have to make himself wait.

He waited seven whole days.

Three days after his meeting with the prayer group, they invited him to a Sunday night potluck supper. Ron went, hoping *she* would be there. She was.

Ron sat at a table across from her. He found they could talk easily and soon they were locked in an animated discussion about themselves and about their Lord.

Marjorie Davis was 34 years old, a single mother whose 10 year old daughter was named Dina. She had been traveling with a woman evangelist, tutoring the woman's children, and had arrived in Salt Lake only a few weeks earlier. Her personality was warm and vivacious, but her soft eyes reminded him of the eyes of a deer, deep and peaceful.

Marge looked as if she had been a believer for her entire life. She had probably been sheltered. She had probably never talked to an ex-pusher or an ex-con.

"I'd like to come and see you this week," Ron told her. But he knew he had to lay all his cards on the table. "That is, if you don't mind being visited by a man who's done a lot of time in the joint. . .uh, in prison I mean."

"I'd love to have you come and see me, Ron," she answered sincerely.

On Wednesday afternoon, Ron knocked on the door of Marge's apartment. He knew that she would be home. His mind had been so consumed with thoughts of her that he had taken the afternoon off work to see her.

She greeted him in blue jeans and a pink plaid shirt, looking even more innocent and young than she had at their first two meetings. His heart pounded in fear. "I should go away," he thought. "I should leave her alone."

But Marge took his arm warmly and sat him at her dining table with a tall glass of iced tea and a platter of cookies. She once more sat across from him, smiling, and their conversation flowed as before.

Ron wanted to tell her about his past. Several times he tried to reveal his sordid history. Yet each time he began, Marge interrupted.

"Ron, if you're trying to 'warn' me about you, I appreciate it," she said finally. "But you don't need to. I think that first you had better hear a little about *my* past."

Marjorie, who seemed so childlike and innocent, who appeared to have been raised as a Christian, shared a story of past bondage that equaled Ron's own. She told of years of communal living in a cave in California.

She told of years of involvment in the occult and the powers she had used to influence people and events. She told of her time in Las Vegas as a call girl. She told of years as a slave to heroin, and of the rebellion that eventually led to the death of her first child.

As she talked, Ron was amazed at the parallels between their lives. This wonderfully tender woman had once been so hardened that she could feel nothing for a man, not even friendship. The freshness that lit her countenance was not inborn—it was newborn! Beautiful, childlike innocence flowed from this woman because she had allowed herself to be cleansed by the Spirit and become a new creature in Christ, with old things passed away.

Ron and Marge had begun talking in the sunlit afternoon, but when they stopped, the light pouring in the window was from a full moon. The events in her past did not cause Ron to draw back from Marge; her story only made Ron love her

Ron, Marjorie and Dina

more. He had never imagined himself capable of so much love and understanding.

Ron stood to leave, but suddenly turned around and took both of Marge's hands in his. His eyes met hers and he struggled to find the right words, tender, words. But the words that burst out of his mouth came out with gruff bluntness.

"Woman, I want you to marry me."

"Oh, no. It sounded like a command," he thought, "and it was too soon." But now his intentions were revealed, so he swallowed and said it once more.

"I want you to marry me."

Her pause seemed like an eternity. Then her eyes twinkled as she replied, "Well, it's about *time* you asked me!!!"

She laughed. And Ron laughed. Then she cried. As he embraced this priceless gift from the Lord, Ron closed his eyes tightly, or he, too, would have started to cry.

The wedding ceremony took place in the little Baptist church. Rev. Jim Powers of the Full Armor Fellowship came over to assist in the ceremony, and communion was served by Marjorie's friend, Rev. Pat Squire.

The service was unusual. Highly unusual. As unusual as their courtship and as their lives. When it was over, Ron lifted his new wife in his arms at the alter and spun her around and around with shouts of joy. New church friends and old 'street' friends clapped and cheered wildly.

As Ron and Marge greeted their guests on the way to their car, a man hugged Ron and slipped a twenty dollar bill into his hand. "I didn't know what wedding present to buy, but my wife and I thought we could give you this to buy a nice meal on your honeymoon. I just wish I had more to give you—this may not be enough."

Ron looked at the twenty in his hand and then thanked the man with a bear-hug. The gift touched him deeply.

"Oh, Brother," Ron smiled, "It will be enough. It's more than enough."

Ron handed the money to Marge and shook his head in wonder.

"This shows the huge difference that knowing Jesus makes in a man's life," he told his bride. "I can look at a mere twenty dollars now and feel so content, and say "it's enough." I was just remembering how just 4 years ago I held a million dollars in my hands and said 'It's *not* enough."

"A million dollars?" Marge gasped. "When did you hold a million dollars?"

"I have a lot of things left to tell you, Mrs. Rearick. But then, we have a whole lifetime to know each other, don't we? A whole eternity . . ."

Appendix I

These are the Scriptures that have brought me to fulfillment in God's family:

"If thou shalt confess with thy mouth the Lord Jesus, and shalt believe in thine heart that God hath raised him from the dead, thou shalt be saved."

Romans 10:9

"If we confess our sins, he is faithful and just to forgive us our sins, and to cleanse us from all unrighteousness."

I John 1:9

". . . but ye have received the Spirit of adoption, whereby we cry Abba Father."

Romans 8:15

"Therefore, if any man be in Christ, he is a new creature. Old things are passed away. Behold, all things are become new."

II Cor. 5:17

"Also I heard the voice of the Lord, saying, whom shall I send, and who will go for us. Then said I, here am I, send me."

Isaiah 6:8

Christ's Disciples, members of the I.C.B.A. (International Christian Bikers Association). . . some real changed lives.

Appendix II

DRUG ABUSE CHART

For use by teachers, pastors, and all others who work with young addicts.

DRUG NAME	COMMON NAMES	POSSIBLE EFFECTS	SIGNS OF OVERDOSE	WITHDRAWAL SYMPTOMS
A. NARCOTICS (natural) opium morphine codeine heroin (synthetic) methadone meperidine	cube, first-line, mud Big H, junk, smack, brown sugar, horse "meth"	euphoria, drowsiness, depression, constricted pupils, nausea, respiratory problems	slow and shallow breathing clammy skin, convulsions, coma, and death	watery eyes, runny nose, yawning, loss of appetite, tremors, chills, panic
B. CANNABIS marijuana hashish hashish oil tetra hydrocannibinol	pot, refer, grass, weed hash, soles	disoriented behavior, relaxed inhibitions, increased appetite	fatigue, paranoia, possible psychosis	insomnia and hyperactivity
C. STIMULANTS cocaine amphetamines phenmetrazine methylphenidate	coke, snow, dust, "C" uppers, bennies, speed, "meth"	increased alertness, euphoria, increased pulse & blood pressure, insomnia, loss of appetite	agitation, increase in body temperature, hallucinations, convulsions, death	apathy, long periods of sleep, irritability, depression, disorientation
C. DEPRESSANTS chloral hydrate barbiturates methaqualine benzodiazophines	barbs, downers blues, reds, yellows, also many trade names such as Valium, Quaalude	drunken behavior, slurred speech, disorientation	cold, clammy skin, weak & rapid pulse, shallow respiration, coma, death	anxiety, insomnia, tremors, delirium, convulsions, death
E. HALLUCIGINATES mescaline & peyote L.S.D. amphetamine variants psilocybin, psilocyn phencyclidine (PCP) DOM, DOB, MDA, MMDA	cactus, button Acid, haze, freeway hit, sunshine (mushrooms) angel dust, crystal "serenity"	illusions, hallucinations, poor perception of time and distance	longer, more intense trips, psychosis, anger and violence, death	none— but flashbacks may occur even after a lengthy time